THE BLACKCAP

HAMLYN SPECIES GUIDES

THE BLACKCAP

C.F. Mason

HAMLYN

First published in 1995 by Hamlyn Limited,
an imprint of Reed Consumer Books Ltd
Michelin House, 81 Fulham Road, London SW3 6RB
and Auckland, Melbourne, Singapore and Toronto

The photographs are reproduced by permission of the following: pp. 14, 15, 42 and 90 David M. Cottridge; pp. 22, 23, 26, 27, 30, 34, 35, 79, 94 and 114 C. F. Mason; p. 67 RSPB/Dusan Boucny; p. 75 RSPB/P. R. Perfect; p. 82 Roger Tidman; back cover RSPB/Mark Hamblin.

ISBN 0 600 58006 7

A CIP catalogue record for this book is available from the British Library

Page design by Jessica Caws
Maps drawn by Louise Griffiths

Printed in Hong Kong

CONTENTS

Series Editor's Foreword 7

1 BLACKCAPS AND
   THEIR ALLIES 8
   Warblers 9
   The genus *Sylvia* 11
   The Blackcap 13
   Breeding distribution 15
   Winter distribution 18

2 BLACKCAP HABITATS 20
   Spring habitats 20
   Population densities 24
   Habitat management and
      change 29
   Habitat outside the
      breeding season 36

3 BLACKCAP
   POPULATIONS 38
   Territory 38
   Territoriality between
      species 42
   Population trends 45
   Mortality 49

4 BREEDING BIOLOGY 54
   Spring arrival 54
   Courtship 57
   The nest 58
   Breeding seasons 60
   Eggs 63

Nestlings 65
Nest protection 66
Productivity 69

5 DIETS AND FORAGING 72
   Spring diets 72
   The switch to fruit 76
   Garden Blackcaps 81

6 BLACKCAP LANGUAGE 85
   Song 85
   Callnotes 90

7 KEEPING IN TRIM 92
   Moult 92
   Weight 97

8 MIGRATION 102
   The stimulus to migrate 103
   Navigation 105
   The east-west divide 106
   Genetical control of
      migration 108
   The journey south 112
   Crossing the desert 113
   Winter movements 117
   Spring migration 117

Bibliography 118

Scientific names 122

Index 124

Acknowledgements

I would like to thank my wife Sheila for her help during all stages of the preparation of this book. Cathy Lowne at Hamlyn provided much patient assistance.

Blackcaps are common birds of Pedunculate Oakwoods, where they glean insects from among the leaves.

Series Editor's Foreword

I have always considered the Blackcap to be one of the finest of Britain's songsters, some individuals perhaps rivalling even the renowned Nightingale. Its song, poured forth from our deciduous woodlands in spring, is a true delight to hear. Even though most do not reach the shores of north-west Europe until April or even early May, this is still one of the earliest summer visitors to arrive back on its breeding grounds, its mellow tones contrasting with the monotonous song of the Chiffchaff, which returns from its wintering grounds a few weeks earlier.

With its striking black cap (rich brown on the female), the Blackcap is one of the easiest warblers to identify. Fortunately for the birdwatcher, numbers of Blackcaps have been increasing steadily over the last couple of decades, unlike those of some other, related species. The reasons for this are explained in convincing fashion in these pages by Dr Mason, who also describes and elucidates the intriguing relationship between the Blackcap and other warblers in the genus *Sylvia*, in particular the Garden Warbler.

Although most warblers breeding in the northern parts of Europe migrate to Africa for the winter, Blackcaps can be found through the entire winter in Britain and Ireland. These wintering birds have grown rapidly in number over the past twenty years, most of them being found in suburban gardens. Many readers will be very surprised to learn that the vast majority are not British or even Scandinavian breeders, but in fact come from central Europe, from the area around western Austria! It is suggested that this recently discovered and initially quite unexpected reversal of the 'normal' migration direction has evolved as a means of improving survival chances, the birds having a shorter distance to fly and an 'easier' life in the relatively hospitable British winter, with ample food provided at bird tables.

Extensive studies under laboratory conditions have revealed much about the migration habits of warblers, and the Blackcap has played its part admirably in helping us to unravel some of the many mysteries still surrounding the incredible journeys that many millions of birds undertake each year. Recent investigations have demonstrated the existence of a genetic factor, involving a time programme and a direction programme, in the control of migration; this enables the young birds both to head the correct way and to change direction *en route* at the correct times.

These are just some of the many fascinating facts revealed by Dr Mason in his summary of the life of this splendid little warbler.

David A. Christie

7

1

BLACKCAPS AND THEIR ALLIES

To birdwatchers in north-west Europe, February heralds the first signs of spring, when woodlands ring with the songs of Great Tits and Nuthatches and the drumming of Great Spotted Woodpeckers. To these are added the voices of Robins, Wrens, Dunnocks and Song and Mistle Thrushes, which brighten all but the bleakest of winter days with their songs. Later in the month, Chaffinches and Blackbirds join the chorus, but it is generally not until the second or third week of March that our first woodland migrant, the Chiffchaff, arrives and not until the first or even second week of April, when woodland floors are carpeted with anemones and other spring flowers, that Blackcaps are first heard, along with Willow Warblers. To me the song of the Willow Warbler, however ardent, is always tinged with melancholy. By contrast, the flutings of Blackcaps are loud, bold, extrovert – very Mediterranean.

Other migrants arrive in our woodlands through April and by early May the tapestry of birdsong is almost complete, only the wheelbarrow-like creaking of Spotted Flycatchers being yet awaited. Not all individuals, however, are on their territories by then, for arrivals take place into early June.

For many fortunate birdwatchers, Blackcaps are no longer only summer visitors. Increasing numbers are present in winter, when their bold, aggressive nature can be witnessed at birdtables. These individuals are not our summer birds, but visitors from the Continent. In a world beset with gloomy predictions on the environment and its inhabitants, the Blackcap is something of a success. Numbers have been increasing steadily over the past three or more decades. The Blackcap's close relatives have not been so fortunate. In particular, the Common Whitethroat went into a spectacular decline in the late 1960s. In this book, the natural history of the Blackcap is described in the context of that of its close relatives, for there are many overlaps in their ecology as well as important differences.

Warblers

Warblers belong to that great order of birds the Passeriformes, or perching birds, which includes more than half of all species. They all have four toes, arranged with three in front and one behind to provide a tight grip on a perch. Songbirds are in the suborder Oscines or Passeres, which includes some 40 families. As well as the characteristic feet, they also have highly developed syrinxes, or voice-boxes. The Old World warblers are often placed within the family Muscicapidae, which includes the thrushes, chats and flycatchers. In this classification they have the status of a subfamily, Sylviinae. They differ, however, from the thrushes and flycatchers in having, among other features, an unspotted juvenile plumage, resembling the adult plumage. A number of taxonomists have thus split the Muscicapidae into several full families, in which the warblers are placed in the Sylviidae, an arrangement followed by *The Birds of the Western Palearctic* (Cramp 1992).

The Sylviidae, as the common familial name suggests, are found mainly in the Old World, with the greatest diversity of species in Africa south of the Sahara. The gnatwrens and gnatcatchers, however, are entirely New World genera (but placed in a different subfamily from typical Old World warblers), while the kinglets occur in both Old and New Worlds. Of the more typical warblers, only the Arctic Warbler is found in North America, with a distinct race (*kennicotti*) breeding in western Alaska but wintering in south Asia. Australia has some eight species of warbler, with two genera (song-larks, and the Spinifex Bird) not represented elsewhere. New Zealand has a single species, the Fernbird, which is unique to those islands.

In total, there are some 60 genera of Old World warblers and approximately 350 species. The precise number will depend on the current predominance of 'splitters' and 'lumpers' in the taxonomic world, while new species are still being found: an expedition to China in 1989 discovered both the Chinese Leaf Warbler and the Hainan Leaf Warbler.

A new taxonomic procedure, DNA hybridization, has recently cast some doubt on the affinities of the Sylviidae. This technique matches the DNA sequences between two samples and provides an assessment of the genetic difference between them. It provides biologists with a molecular clock to supplement analyses based on morphological or fossil data. It assumes that the differences in sequences between the same genes and proteins in two species have accumulated since the species diverged from a common ancestor, and that the rates at which differences accumulate are constant. The greater the differences

in sequences, the less closely related are the two species. The results have suggested that most typical genera in the Sylviidae are rather distantly related to the genus *Sylvia*, which is considered more closely allied to babblers, while the grass warblers of Africa and the kinglets are thought to be so distantly related as to be placed in separate families. This technique, however, remains controversial.

Old World warblers are typically of small or very small size, generally plainly coloured, and with fine, narrowly pointed bills. They have ten primary wing feathers, in contrast to the New World warblers (Parulidae) which have only nine. In the majority of species there are no major differences in plumage between males and females, the Blackcap being one striking exception. Warblers are mostly arboreal, although some species live in vegetation close to the ground, and are insectivorous, although some species also eat fruit and other vegetable matter. Many members of the family are exceedingly difficult to tell apart, even when in the hand. A valuable identification guide to the species occurring in the Western Palearctic is that of Parmenter and Byers (1991), while Simms (1985) provides an overview of the group.

The genus *Sylvia*

A fossil *Sylvia* warbler from France has shown the genus to be at least 20 million years old. The genus comprises the typical or scrub warblers, with a centre of distribution in the maquis or evergreen-scrub zone of the Mediterranean, hence the common name. Seventeen species of *Sylvia* are generally recognized, four of which, however, have no Mediterranean populations. The Desert Warbler lives in open deserts and on arid hillsides with low vegetation and scattered bushes; it is found in the western Sahara, including parts of Morocco and Algeria, and in central Asia, east and south of the Caspian Sea. Tristram's Warbler also occurs in Morocco and Algeria but in the Atlas Mountains, mainly above 1000 m, in scrub with Juniper and Evergreen Oak. Ménétries's Warbler inhabits scrub and small thickets, gardens and riverbanks, being distributed in eastern Turkey, northern Iran and around the Caspian, with small populations in Syria and Iraq. The Arabian Warbler lives in thorn scrub in semi-deserts, mainly on the coasts of the southern Red Sea but with a small population in Israel from south of the Dead Sea to Eilat.

Sylvia warblers breeding in Britain; Blackcap (male and female); Garden Warbler; Whitethroat; Dartford Warbler and Lesser Whitethroat.

Of the remaining 13 species, six have a range restricted to the Mediterranean. The most widely distributed is the Sardinian Warbler, breeding from Portugal to Turkey, Israel, the Maghreb and northern Libya, that is wherever maquis is found. The Subalpine Warbler is limited to the western and central Mediterranean, but it has a wider occurrence within Iberia than the Sardinian Warbler. The Spectacled Warbler is more typical of low scrub (garrigue) and has a largely western Mediterranean range, not occurring further east than Italy, apart from populations on Cyprus and in Israel. Both Sardinian and Spectacled Warblers are also found on the Canary Islands, while the latter extends to Madeira and the Cape Verde Islands. Marmora's Warbler inhabits south-eastern Spain and the Balearic Islands, where it is locally common on Mallorca in coastal maquis, whereas on Corsica and Sardinia it is found on mountain slopes to 900 m. The Cyprus Warbler is endemic to that island, where it is common in most areas with dense scrub. The handsome Rüppell's Warbler ranges from southern Greece, through the Aegean islands and southern Turkey to Lebanon. The harsh churrings of all of these scrub warblers are the characteristic sound of the Mediterranean maquis, but the birds are very difficult to spot as they flit rapidly from one patch of dense vegetation to the next.

The Orphean Warbler is also Mediterranean in its western range, but there is an eastern subspecies which breeds discontinuously from Turkey and Israel across to Afghanistan. Of the six more widely occurring species, the Dartford Warbler has the most restricted distribution: it is found in the coastal Maghreb of North Africa, throughout Iberia, western France into southern England, southern France, the coastal belt of Italy, and on the islands of Corsica, Sardinia and Sicily. In contrast, the Barred Warbler has an easterly range, breeding mainly from eastern Europe and across Russia into the Eastern Palearctic. The Lesser Whitethroat also has an easterly distribution, Britain being the north-western limit of its range, and it does not breed in western France or Iberia. There are two subspecies of Lesser Whitethroat in central Asia, Hume's Lesser Whitethroat (*althaea*) and Desert Lesser Whitethroat (*minula*), which are given full species status by some taxonomists.

Of the three remaining species, the Garden Warbler does not breed in the Mediterranean zone but extends north to the forest edge in Sweden and Finland and across into the Eastern Palearctic. The common Whitethroat and the Blackcap have breeding populations in the Mediterranean, including the coastal Maghreb of North Africa, but they do not extend as far north into Scandinavia as the Garden Warbler.

These contrasting distribution patterns are matched by a diversity of migration strategies (Berthold 1988b). Two species, Barred Warbler and Garden Warbler are exclusively long-distance migrants. Five species are middle-distance migrants: Subalpine Warbler, Orphean Warbler, Common Whitethroat, Lesser Whitethroat and Rüppell's Warbler. Barred Warbler, Garden Warbler and Common Whitethroat are also regular transequatorial migrants. The remaining species are short-to-middle-distance migrants, several having evolved populations which are fully resident, including the British Dartford Warbler. The Blackcap has populations which together exhibit all of the characteristics of the migration strategies of the other species. Thus, those on the Cape Verde Islands, and possibly other Atlantic islands, are resident; northern European populations are long-distance migrants, many crossing the equator; while most Atlantic and Mediterranean populations are short-distance or partial migrants.

The Blackcap

The Blackcap is obviously named from the colour of the male's crown. The scientific name is similarly derived, *Sylvia* meaning a wood, *ater* black and *capillus* the hair of the head. Francesca Greenoak, in her book *All the Birds of the Air*, lists a dozen local English names for the species, four of which refer to the black crown. The bird has been called both King Harry Black Cap and Black-headed Hay-jack in Norfolk, Black-headed Peggy ('peggy' being a general term for warblers) and, in North Yorkshire, Coal Hoodie. Four names refer to the choice of nesting materials: Jack Straw, a Somerset name, and, from Northamptonshire, Hay Bird, Hay Chat and Hay Jack. The fluting song has given rise to the names Mock Nightingale and Northern Nightingale, while Blackcaps are also called Nettle Creepers and Nettle Mongers, nettly names being given to several other warblers.

While many warbler species are rather difficult to tell apart, the Blackcap is

Early Blackcap singing from flowering Sallow.

Male Blackcap showing the diagnostic black cap, relatively thick bill and rather plain, unmarked plumage.

easy. The male has that distinctive glossy black cap, extending to eye level. Sardinian and Orphean Warblers also have black caps, but these are more extensive, while their white outer tail feathers are a further distinguishing feature, for white is entirely lacking in the Blackcap's tail. The black cap contrasts well with an ashy-grey face and neck. The chin and throat are often silvery, while the breast is a pale ash-grey, the lower breast and belly being a dull white. The upperparts are a greyish olive-brown and the wing feathers greyish-black, as are the tail feathers.

The female is equally distinctive, with a rich reddish-brown cap. The body is browner, less grey, than the male's but the wings and tail are the same greyish-black. The juveniles resemble the female in colour but are often browner. The crown of the juvenile male is more blackish-brown than that of the adult female, while juvenile females have a more yellowish-brown crown. Young males in the autumn often have some brown feathers mixed in with the black. Blackcaps have a black bill, dark grey legs and brown eyes.

With a total length of 14 cm, the Blackcap is slightly smaller than a sparrow. The average wing length is 74 mm, but varies among populations. The wing is longer and more pointed in northern populations, which are known to be more migratory, while southern populations, such as those of Gibraltar and Sicily,

The Sardinian Warbler also has a black cap but this extends below the red eye. Note also the white outer-tail feathers, absent in the Blackcap.

which are thought to be resident, have shorter, more rounded wings. In Sicily, an altitudinal difference has also been found (Lo Valvo *et al.* 1988): Blackcaps breeding at 1700 m on the slopes of Mount Etna have a mean wing length of 70 mm, compared with 66 mm for coastal populations. Presumably, the montane Blackcaps move to winter quarters at lower altitudes.

Garden Warblers, although they have the same average breeding-season weight as Blackcaps of 30 g, have an average wing length of 77 mm, some 3 mm longer than Blackcaps. They migrate, of course, over longer distances.

Blackcaps and Garden Warblers are the shortest-legged of the *Sylvia* warblers, the Garden Warbler having a slightly shorter tarsus than its congener. Short legs are an adaptation to an arboreal way of life. The Blackcap's bill is slightly longer, narrower and shallower than that of the Garden Warbler.

Breeding distribution

Five races, or subspecies, of the Blackcap are currently recognized, although clinal variation occurs and subspecies recognition is often very subjective. The breeding distribution is shown in Fig. 1.1 and lies largely within the 14 °C–30 °C July isotherms. The nominate

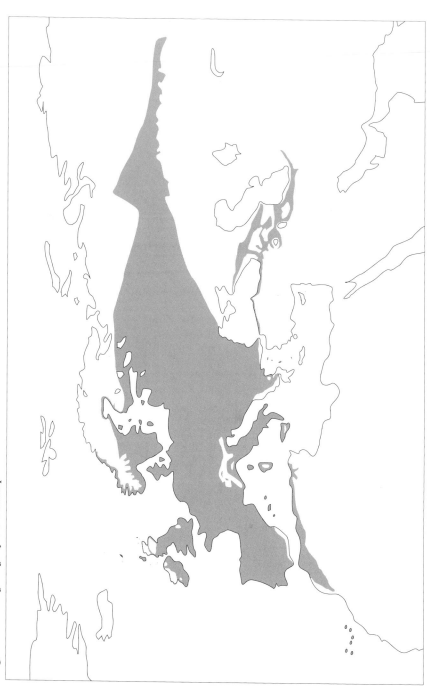

Fig. 1.1 *Breeding range of the Blackcap*

race, *Sylvia atricapilla atricapilla*, occurs across Europe and western Siberia, extending in range in a narrow finger just to the east of Novosibirsk. In the north, Blackcaps breed in Norway, mainly in the lowland areas near the coast, across southern and central Sweden, in southern Finland and across the forest belt of Russia; unlike Garden Warblers, they do not extend further north into the subarctic birch zone. The southern edge of the breeding range of the nominate race is the Pyrenees, northern Italy, the Balkans, Greece and the Black Sea coast of Turkey, extending to the west and north of the Black Sea but excluding the Crimea. Blackcaps breed at altitudes of up to 1400 m in the Alps. In Greece, this is a bird of montane forests and has recently colonized the Peloponnese in the south of the country, where it is found mainly in sub-montane and montane forest between 700 m and 1480 m (Hölzinger 1990). Some individuals summer in Cyprus and Israel, but there is no proof of breeding there.

The race *dammholzi* has greyer upperparts and paler underparts than the nominate race, with more white on the belly. The population is isolated from that of nominate *atricapilla*, occurring in the Caucasus Mountains of Georgia, where it breeds at up to 2000 m, in neighbouring Armenia, Azerbaijan, north-eastern and eastern Turkey, and in northern Iran in the Elburz Mountains between the Caspian Sea and the capital, Tehran.

On the Balearic Islands, Corsica, Sardinia, in Tunisia, central Italy and, perhaps, southern Italy and Sicily is the race *pauluccii*, which is more greyish-olive, less brown, than the nominate race. The race *heineken* breeds in Madeira, the Canary Islands, Portugal, western and south-western Spain, and possibly elsewhere in Spain, Morocco and Algeria. It is smaller and darker than other Blackcaps, but the imprecise knowledge of its distribution indicates that these races are not easily told apart and there are individual birds of intermediate appearance. The final race, *gularis*, is very similar to the nominate race but has a longer bill and shorter wings. It is restricted to the Azores and Cape Verde Islands in the Atlantic Ocean, the latter archipelago lying south of the Tropic of Cancer and holding the only tropical breeding population of Blackcaps.

During the fieldwork in 1968–72 for the British Trust for Ornithology's (BTO) *Atlas of Breeding Birds in Britain and Ireland* (Sharrock 1976), the Blackcap was found in 59 per cent of 10-km squares. Willow Warbler, Goldcrest, Common Whitethroat, Chiffchaff, Sedge Warbler and Grasshopper Warbler were all more widely distributed warbler species, mainly because they were more widespread in Ireland. The new *Atlas*, based on fieldwork in 1988–91 (Gibbons *et al.* 1993), has shown an expansion in range, Blackcaps now occurring in 64 per cent of the total 10-km squares. There has been a 6.5 per cent increase in the number of squares occupied in Britain and a 39.5 per cent increase in Ireland.

Blackcaps breed through most of England and Wales, being absent only from the treeless fens and from the moorland hilltops of Wales and the Pennines. They even nest within the Royal Parks of central London. The new *Atlas* provides an estimate of abundance, and shows the greatest density to be south of a line from South Wales to the Wash.

In Scotland, Blackcaps have become increasingly widespread since the 1970s. They are generally distributed, if in small numbers, in woodlands north to the central lowlands, but more thinly in Argyll, Perth and Angus. They breed in small numbers on the east coast to Aberdeen and on the south side of the Moray Firth, as well as in Inverness and Ross and Cromarty. Singing males penetrate as far as Sutherland and Caithness, but without evidence of nesting. There are occasional breeding records from Orkney, Shetland and the Hebrides (Thom 1986).

Blackcaps are locally distributed in Ireland, but there has been a recent spread towards the west of the country, with breeding records in Mayo, Galway and western Clare where there were none in the early 1970s.

Winter distribution

Large numbers of Blackcaps winter in the western and central Mediterranean region, south to the northern edge of the Sahara Desert. Rather fewer are present in winter in the eastern Mediterranean region such as the coastal areas of Greece and Turkey and in Egypt and Libya. Blackcaps are locally common in winter in West Africa, especially in the westernmost countries of Mauritania, Senegal, the Gambia and Guinea. They are also locally common in East Africa, for example in Ethiopia, southern Sudan, Uganda, Kenya and Tanzania, with smaller numbers south to eastern Zaire and Malawi. The race *dammholzi* winters in east and north-east Africa and occurs together with the nominate race, in some areas as in the Kenyan highlands (Pearson 1978). There are probably fewer wintering Blackcaps elsewhere in Africa, although they may be more widespread on migration. There is a single record from the Transvaal of South Africa.

It has generally been considered that the majority of Blackcaps winter in the Mediterranean region, but this view may be biased because there are more observers in that region and also a considerable hunting pressure: many ringed birds are recovered there having been killed by man, compared with few in sub-Saharan Africa. It is not known what proportion of Blackcaps migrates across the Sahara to winter in Africa, or whether the proportion varies between years, or whether individual populations or individuals consistently winter north or south of the desert.

There have been records of Blackcaps wintering in Britain for well over a century, Morris (1860) listing birds from Worcester, Kent, Surrey, Norfolk and Yorkshire, as well as several from Ireland. The rapidly increasing winter population is, however, a new phenomenon. In the 1940s and 1950s there was an average of 22 Blackcaps recorded in county bird reports each winter, while during the 1970s the annual average was 380. A special survey in the winter of 1978/79 revealed 1714 Blackcaps (Leach 1981). The BTO's *Atlas of Wintering Birds in Britain and Ireland* (Lack 1986) illustrated the distribution of Blackcaps in the early 1980s. They were quite widely distributed, but there was a preponderance of birds in the Midlands, the south-west (especially each side of the Bristol Channel) and in southern and south-central England. Nevertheless, there was a scattering of observations into Scotland, including Orkney and Shetland, where Blackcaps only rarely breed. They were annual visitors to a large, urban garden in Aberdeen as early as 1965, when up to three were present at any one time (A. Macdonald, pers. comm.); they would tap on the kitchen window to be fed! In the early 1980s, it was estimated that up to 3000 Blackcaps wintered each year in the British Isles; rather more probably do so now. Increases in wintering Blackcaps have also been recorded in Belgium (Fouarge 1981a) and the Netherlands.

Most Blackcaps winter in gardens, and the highest numbers are recorded in January and February. It might be thought that these winter Blackcaps are British birds which no longer migrate south, but, in fact, they are probably all of Continental origin, breeding in southern Germany and Austria. There have been 95 recoveries in winter of Blackcaps ringed on the Continent during the breeding season but no winter recoveries of British breeders (Berthold and Terrill 1988). Possible reasons for this change in migratory behaviour are discussed in Chapter 8.

2

BLACKCAP HABITATS

The Blackcap is primarily a breeding bird of mature deciduous-forest habitats, but the other three summer-visiting *Sylvia* warblers in Britain are also basically woodland birds. All four may hold territories in the same wood. Species with similar ecology cannot live together in the same habitat, a concept known as the 'principle of competitive exclusion'. Closely related species will coexist only if they occupy different niches. An ecological niche is defined as the place of an organism in the biotic environment, and its relation to food and enemies (Elton 1927). The niche therefore defines the role of an animal in its environment.

Sylvia warblers could coexist in an area by having slightly different habitat preferences. They could occur in the same place but exploit different vertical zones of the habitat, one species, for example, feeding in the canopy and the other in the shrub layer. Alternatively, they could actively compete for space and hold mutually exclusive territories. We must also remember that components of the niche may be rather fluid entities. In the absence of competitors, or when densities are low, the range of habitats occupied by a species may be quite broad. When populations are high and competitive interactions likely, the species may retreat into that habitat within which it is best adapted and competitively superior, what we can call its habitat refuge (Edington and Edington 1972).

Spring habitats

The most favoured habitats for Blackcaps are mature deciduous or mixed woodlands with a well-developed shrub layer. The shrub layer is important for Blackcaps, so they are much scarcer in western oak woods, which are habitually grazed by sheep, than they are in ungrazed eastern woods (Simms 1971). They will also breed in overgrown hedgerows, especially if these contain tall trees, as well as in scrubby areas and in shrubberies in well-established parks and gardens, even in urban areas. Tall trees are used as songposts and are an essential component of the habitat.

Table 2.1. *Percentage distribution of nests within major habitat types.*

	Blackcap	Garden Warbler	Whitethroat	Lesser Whitethroat
Deciduous woodland	76.4	61.7	18.8	17.1
Coniferous woodland	1.7	1.6	3.1	0.3
Scrub	3.7	24.9	55.7	33.9
Hedgerows	5.0	2.6	17.7	39.7
Parks	11.7	8.2	4.7	6.5
Other habitats	1.5	0.9	0	2.4
Total nests	785	546	3040	292

An analysis of the BTO's nest record cards provided information on the proportion of nests found within major habitat types (Mason 1976). There may be some bias in where observers search for nests, but the results broadly indicate the breeding habitats of Blackcaps in Britain. As any biases will be the same for all *Sylvia* species, the results will highlight any differences in habitat selection between them. The findings, given in Table 2.1, show that the great majority of Blackcaps are found in mature deciduous woodland. Garden Warblers occur much more in scrub habitats, but there is considerable overlap between the two species. The whitethroats are predominantly scrub and hedgerow birds, the Common Whitethroat being more frequent in scrub and the Lesser Whitethroat in hedgerows. Similar results have been obtained from detailed habitat studies in both northern England and southern Sweden, with Blackcap and Garden Warbler having the most similar habitat requirements (Cody 1978).

The relationship between vegetation structure and the distribution of *Sylvia* warblers has also been examined in Sardinia (Cody and Walter 1976), where six species occur: these are Spectacled, Marmora's, Dartford, Sardinian, Subalpine and Blackcap, the first-mentioned being very scarce. Blackcaps preferred the tallest habitat with a high density of vegetation at the greatest heights; in other words, a well-developed canopy with sparser vegetation at lower levels. Spectacled, Marmora's and Dartford Warblers occupied low scrub habitats, while Sardinian and Subalpine Warblers were intermediate. There was considerable overlap between Subalpine Warbler and Blackcap, as there is between Blackcap and Garden Warbler in northern Europe. On Sardinia, breeding Blackcaps occupied tall maquis, scrub woodland, Evergreen Oak woods and montane coniferous forests, in the last of which they were the only

21

Blackcaps will nest in large, mature gardens, such as this one with a pond, small wildflower meadow and hedgerow of native shrubs.

Sylvia. Similar habitats are occupied in Iberia, Italy and Greece, but citrus groves are apparently preferred to some natural woods in Sicily (Massa 1981). Native coniferous woodland is occupied in many areas of mainland Europe.

In Britain, Blackcaps appear most associated with woods of Pedunculate Oak but they also frequent woods dominated by Ash, Beech, Alder and Sweet Chestnut, while some Highland birch woods have them. The shrub layer is the most important component of the woodland.

Blackcaps are generally uncommon in mature conifer plantations, even when suitable understorey exists. In Buckinghamshire, a 14-year-old stand of Japanese Larch had 18 per cent of songposts, compared with 82 per cent in the adjacent mixed woodland (Williamson 1971a). However, if conifer plantations are of mixed age and some broadleaved trees are present, for example as a screen, Blackcaps will hold territories.

Alder carr, a successional woodland habitat such aas this in Norfolk Broadland, holds good numbers of Blackcaps.

Blackcaps nest in coniferous woodland in the Alps.

The size of deciduous woodland appears to have little influence on the presence of Blackcaps. Of 76 woods larger than 20 ha, all contained the species, while it was present in more than 80 per cent of woods smaller than 20 ha (Fuller 1982). In an Oxfordshire study Blackcaps occurred in the majority of woods, which ranged in size from 0.1 to 18 ha (Ford 1987). In a survey of 36 woodlands and woodland fragments in north-east Essex in 1994 I found Blackcaps in all but five. All but one of the negative woods was smaller than 0.5 ha. Most spinneys and shelterbelts within farmland will hold Blackcaps, and farms with some woodland have twice as many pairs as those without (Lack 1989). Blackcaps, and indeed a number of other species, tend to be more numerous near the edge than in the interior of woods.

Population densities

Blackcaps hold a prominent position in many woodland bird assemblages. In a survey of 88 Pedunculate Oak woods in England, the Blackcap was found to be, overall, the eleventh most abundant breeding species, making up 2 per cent of the bird community, as determined by song registrations. The most abundant species were Chaffinch, Robin, Wren, Blackbird and Willow Warbler, while Garden Warblers were marginally more numerous than Blackcaps in this study (Simms 1971). In Sessile Oak woods Blackcaps did not

24

feature in the top 15 species, probably because of the lack of a dense shrub layer owing to sheep grazing. In studies of individual English lowland woods, Blackcaps ranged from the sixth to the tenth commonest species (Parsons 1976; Fuller and Henderson 1992), while they made up 4 per cent of the bird community of a Yew wood (Williamson and Williamson 1973). The species is poorly represented in scrub (Morgan 1975).

In southern Europe, Blackcaps often make up a greater proportion of the woodland bird assemblage. In coastal woodland in Tuscany, they were the most numerous species, followed by Wrens. In coastal oak woods near Rome they were second only to Nightingales, making up 16 per cent of the total passerine community, while in high forest near Pisa only Robins and Wrens were more numerous (Lambertini 1981; Farina 1982; Fraticelli and Sarrocco 1984). In Galicia, north-west Spain, Blackcaps were second only to Wrens in 13-year-old plantations of alien *Eucalyptus*, but they were only of sixth importance in younger plantations; the shrub layers were very similar in height and density in both plantations, despite the difference in age. In the same area Blackcaps were the fifth most dominant species in native

Blackaps can be abundant in plantations of Eucalyptus, widely introduced for forestry in Spain.

This small spinney, on a traffic island in Suffolk, held a Blackcap territory in 1993. Note the colony of Pyramidal Orchids.

deciduous woods but only twelfth in Maritime Pine (Bongiorno 1982). In Spanish habitats bordering the Strait of Gibraltar, Blackcaps were the third-dominant species in undisturbed oak woods, surpassed only by Chaffinch and Bonelli's Warbler, but they did not occur in disturbed woods. They were also among the dominants (sixth position), though less numerous, in mature pine woods. In Mediterranean bushlands (maquis or matorral), three *Sylvia* warblers, Dartford, Sardinian and Blackcap, comprised up to 60 per cent of the bird community, with 32 per cent of total birds at one locality being Blackcaps (Finlayson 1992).

The data collected for the Common Birds Census (CBC) of the BTO indicate an average Blackcap density of 15.1 pairs per sq km in British woodlands. Of the warblers, only the Willow Warbler is more numerous, with a density of almost three times as many pairs (Hickling 1983). Much higher Blackcap densities have been recorded from individual woodland sites, although they may, of course, fluctuate widely from year to year. Thus, lime woods in

Riverine woodland in Lithuania, where Blackcaps share habitat with Common Rosefinches, Thrush Nightingales and Golden Orioles.

Lincolnshire held 200 pairs per sq km (Fuller and Whittington 1987), a coppice wood in Suffolk 40 pairs per sq km (Fuller and Henderson 1992) and a mixed wood in Somerset 130 pairs per sq km (Parsons 1976). The average density in 36 woods and woodland fragments in north-east Essex in 1994, not a particularly good Blackcap year, was 56 pairs/sq km. In scrub habitats densities are much lower, of the order of three–nine pairs per sq km (Morgan 1975; Williamson 1975). Restocked conifer plantations in Wales had an average of 16 pairs per sq km (Bibby *et al.* 1985).

In Sweden, Blackcap densities average four pairs per sq km in coniferous woodland and 25–38 per sq km in deciduous woodland (Ulfstrand and Högstedt 1976; Nilsson 1977). Rich riverine forest in Germany held 100 pairs per sq km (Gnielka 1987). In southern Europe densities are generally higher, with, for example, 200–300 pairs per sq km in Sardinia and 166 in coastal oak forest in Italy, but only 26.3 pairs per sq km in mature pine forest (Fraticelli and Sarrocco 1984; Farina 1982). In Italy, densities are frequently of the order of 500–900 pairs per sq km in the most suitable habitats (Baldeschi 1981).

Interesting data have been collected in the Białowieza National Park in Poland, one of the few areas of Europe considered still to be in its primeval state. In plots of coniferous or mixed forest Blackcaps averaged about three pairs per sq km, being the seventeenth most abundant species. In oak–Hornbeam plots there were 13–28 pairs per sq km, while in Ash–Alder plots or Alder swamps there were 31–49 pairs and Blackcaps were the fifth most abundant species (Tomialojc *et al.* 1984). Densities generally appear on the low side compared with managed woodland plots.

The numbers of Blackcaps, and indeed of many other primarily woodland or scrub species, on farmland will depend on the proportion of woodland, including shelterbelts, spinneys and overgrown hedgerows. For example, an estate in Essex, extending over 700 ha, contained only 11 per cent of woodland, but this held 30 per cent of the breeding pairs of the farm's 50 species of birds (Mason and Long 1987). In Switzerland, the ideal farmland habitat for Blackcaps was when hedges occupied 4 per cent of the total area (60–80 m of hedge per ha) and no fields were more than 300 m across (Pfister *et al.* 1986). The Essex farm had 56 m of hedgerow per ha, with rather larger field sizes.

On a Norfolk farm, Blackcaps were twenty-fifth in terms of abundance (Bull *et al.* 1976). In the Cambridgeshire parish of Hilton they made up 0.3 per cent of the bird community, most pairs being associated with large trees within the village (Wyllie

1976). Overall on CBC plots, Blackcaps made up 0.7 per cent of the total farmland pairs (Shrubb 1970).

Blackcaps have an overall density of 2.2 pairs per sq km on farmland, some seven times less than on woodland plots. The average density on farmland with and without some woodland is 2.88 and 1.40 territories per sq km respectively (Lack 1989). Densities per sq km in individual study areas holding Blackcaps ranged from 0.7 pairs in Cambridgeshire to 6.7 pairs in Suffolk and 8.2 pairs in Dorset (Wyllie 1976; Benson and Williamson 1972; Williamson 1971b). Densities on farmland in north-west Spain were much higher, at 28 pairs per sq km, but farming in this area was small-scale with a very high frequency (180 m/ha) of tall hedges (Bongiorno 1982).

Habitat management and change

Virtually none of the woodland remaining in Britain can be considered natural, that is untouched by the hand of man. Indeed, the majority of woodland has been managed for a very long time. The destruction of the original forest cover that developed after the last ice age began in the Neolithic, some 3000 years BC and continued throughout the Bronze Age. Areas such as the East Anglian Brecks were cleared as early as the Neolithic, and our Bronze Age ancestors began to clear forest from upland areas. A detailed study is provided by Rackham (1976), who also discusses how the essential elements of our modern landscape – the patterns of woodland, farmland and villages – were, by the early part of the thirteenth century, very much as they are now in appearance. The management of woodlands probably began in Roman and Anglo-Saxon times, but by the Middle Ages the majority of woods were being managed.

Woodland management in lowland England was largely as coppice-with-standards. The majority of trees were cut to the ground at intervals (coppiced) and allowed to regrow from the stool, while a scattering of trees, especially oaks, was left to grow on to maturity (the standards). The coppice (or underwood) was cut in rotation, from five to 20 years depending on species and site, so that different compartments of the wood would be at different stages of growth, providing a range of densities and heights of vegetation as a mosaic within the wood. The coppice wood had a whole variety of uses, as firewood, fencing, building material and for implements, and nothing of the underwood was wasted, not even the twigs and trimmings. The standards provided timbers for houses and ships.

Dense hedgerows, with standard trees, such as this by the Stour in Suffolk, support Blackcap territories, especially in years when populations are high.

This management of woodlands persisted well into the last century and a feeling of the annual cycle of work carried out by the woodsmen can be found in Thomas Hardy's *The Woodlanders*. However the coming of the railways, allowing the transport of coal to industrial areas and the development of the steel industry, led to the decline of coppicing in many areas. Woods fell into disuse and became overgrown and derelict. Unfortunately such woods do not return to their natural, wildwood state, because the density of coppice poles casts a much greater shade, even in winter and early spring, than do high forest trees.

Over the past 30 years, some of our woods have been brought back into coppice management, mostly on nature reserves. The main reasons are to promote the ground flora and also butterflies which can have very precise habitat requirements. Modern coppicing differs in several ways from traditional manage-ment. Many fewer people are involved and modern equipment is used, including tractors and lorries, rather than horses, to remove the

Several species of Sylvia warbler live in close proximity in scrubland habitats in the Mediterranean region. they band to forage at different heights (p. 75) but there are many aggressive interactions (p. 45): Blackcap; Subalpine Warbler, Sardinian Warbler (male); Marmora's Warbler; Spectacled Warbler and Sardinian Warbler (female).

woodcrop. The brush and twigs have no modern use and are usually either burned on site or piled into heaps and left to rot. I would also imagine that the traditional woodsman, who worked all year in his wood, would have controlled bramble growth, which in some coppices today grows so densely as to make the wood impenetrable (Mason and Long 1987).

How does this intensive woodland management influence bird populations, especially those of Blackcaps and their relatives? It is only recently that there have been any investigations. The distribution of songbirds has been studied within mixed coppice stands in the Ham Street National Nature Reserve in Kent (Fuller *et al.* 1989). The underwood was mainly Hornbeam, with Hazel, Sweet Chestnut, Birch, Ash and Maple, with standards of Pedunculate Oak. All migrant species of bird were found to reach their highest densities in the first ten years of coppice growth, in contrast to resident species, which either showed no particular preference with

Young coppice can support high densities of Blackcaps and other migrant songbirds.

regard to coppice age or peaked in numbers when the coppice canopy closed. Blackcaps, together with Nightingales and Chiffchaffs, peaked in the sixth year of coppice growth, whereas Common Whitethroats established in the youngest coppice and disappeared when canopy closure exceeded 50 per cent, in the seventh year. Garden Warblers peaked in numbers after Common Whitethroats, and remained abundant until just after canopy closure. The distribution of the *Sylvia* warblers within coppice thus reflects the broad habitat differences described at the beginning of this chapter. In Ham Street Woods, Blackcaps appeared to be especially associated with the edges of coppice, as did other migrant species, whereas the residents did not show such a preference for edges.

A similar study was carried out in Longbeech Wood, a Sweet Chestnut coppice only 20 km from Ham Street (Fuller and Moreton 1987). There were striking differences in the bird community, and Blackcaps were too scarce for any preferences in coppice age to be detected. This may be because Sweet Chestnut, which almost certainly was introduced by the Romans, carries a smaller insect fauna than native trees do, or because the dense shade cast by chestnut coppice severely reduces the shrub layer. Nevertheless, the scarcity of Blackcaps in this study was surprising, because in Stour Wood, my local wood in north-east Essex, which is largely Sweet Chestnut coppice with many mature chestnut standards, the species is the most numerous warbler.

Bradfield Woods, now managed by the Suffolk Wildlife Trust, have a documented history of coppicing dating back to 1252. In this mixed coppice, both Blackcap and Garden Warbler numbers peaked during canopy closure, five to seven years after coppicing. Garden Warbler numbers then declined sharply and they were not found in coppice of more than 14 years old, but Blackcaps declined more slowly and they were still represented in the oldest coppice. By contrast Common Whitethroats were not found in coppice older than six years (Fuller and Henderson 1992).

Blackcaps, then, appear to be most numerous in coppice of around six years, when the canopy is closing, but is this the best habitat for Blackcaps? We need to know that they settle here preferentially over adjacent habitats of different age and that they are more productive in such habitats, that is that they leave more surviving young. Blackcaps are also characteristic birds of secondary woodland, where the trees are largely mature and even-aged. How do their densities and breeding success differ in the two habitat types?

Fuller (1992) provides an excellent review of our current knowledge of the effects of coppice management on bird communities.

Chestnut coppice, Stour Wood RSPB reserve, north-east Essex, supports good numbers of Blackcaps. (OPPOSITE ABOVE) *Newly coppiced woodland, carpeted with wood anemones, in April when Blackcaps arrive,* (OPPOSITE BELOW) *regrowth in June from stools coppiced the previous winter,* (ABOVE) *three-year coppice, with a dense undergrowth of brambles, providing ideal Blackcap habitat.*

He recommends that, to manage a coppice for warblers, a short rotation of 12 years will achieve the largest populations but it is impracticable to manage an entire wood on short rotation. A split rotation, with part of the wood on a 12-year cycle and the remainder on a 20–25-year-cycle, would substantially increase warbler populations. Rotations longer than 30 years would result in a marked decrease in numbers.

The great interest in describing the conservation benefits of coppicing has meant that other forms of woodland management have received little study. In particular, plantation woodlands have been largely ignored. This is a pity, for the new initiatives for farm woodlands, and the more ambitious proposals for community forests, will undoubtedly involve largely hardwood plantations, albeit of (it is hoped) a diversity of species. In France, densities of Blackcaps were generally higher in coppice-with-standards than in shelterwood, though there was considerable overlap (Ferry and Frochot 1970). In north east Spain, densities in 13-year-old *Eucalyptus* plantations were similar to those in native oak woods (Bongiorno 1982).

Habitat outside the breeding season

On migration Blackcaps frequent more varied habitats, including reedbeds and fens, but nevertheless they select specific habitats just as they do in the breeding season. At a ringing station at Lake Constance, Germany, it was found that immature Blackcaps occurred more often in open scrub habitats, the adults preferring tall thickets of Alder Buckthorn and a small wet Alder wood. Their preference for dense scrub increased as the migration season progressed, some 16 per cent of Blackcaps using it in July and August but 40 per cent during October (Barlein 1983). It was suggested that this change in habitat was due to the shift in diet from insects to berries during the summer (*see* Chapter 5).

Migrants appear to be able to assess the suitability of habitat as they fly over at night. The few birds that descend during the night into unsuitable habitats, areas without significant food, leave quickly at dawn. Males are more likely than females to come down and remain in unsuitable habitats (Herremans 1989).

Some 95 per cent of Blackcaps wintering in Britain are found in gardens, 76 per cent of them in town gardens, and the majority below 100 m (Leach 1981). While Blackcaps in gardens are more easily spotted, the preference for this habitat is undoubtedly genuine, for wintering Chiffchaffs are recorded almost exclusively in rural localities. A party of Blackcaps, three males and a female, wintering in Lancashire, spent most of the time feeding on berries of Sea Buckthorn in a sand dune (Carah 1961); they formed a close group, and left the area only after thrushes had stripped the plants of berries.

Large numbers of Blackcaps winter in the Mediterranean basin, where they inhabit scrublands and olive orchards. They may occur alone or in small flocks and tend to be nomadic, depending on the availability of food. Nevertheless, at least some return to the same wintering area each year, a few having been recaptured up to five years after ringing (Cuadrado 1992). Similar site-fidelity has been recorded in Britain and on Gibraltar. On Gibraltar Blackcaps are solitary, and they may defend a territory with a good fruit supply for several weeks; midwinter densities are typically of

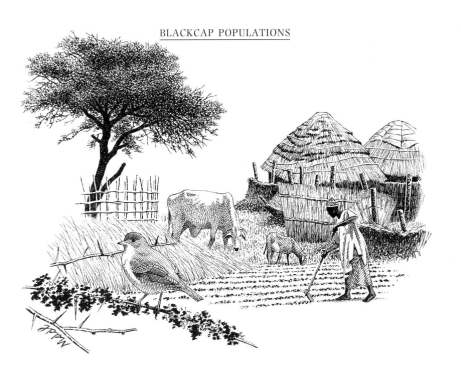

Blackcaps winter on the edges of cultivations in the Gambia.

500 per sq km, numbers doubling in March when migrants pass through (Finlayson 1992). In southern Spain, densities were of up to 300 per sq km in olive plantations and 740 in scrubland (Rodriguez de los Santos *et al.* 1986).

An unknown proportion of Blackcaps winters south of the Sahara, and this may vary depending on the abundance of fruits in the Mediterranean. In West Africa, they winter commonly in acacia scrub, savannah and rainforests, as well as in cultivations and gardens, numbers fluctuating in relation to local fruit supplies (Morel and Morel 1992). They are common in mangroves in the Gambia. In East Africa, Blackcaps are common in montane forests above 2000 m (Pearson and Lack 1992), sometimes up to 3600 m. Garden Warblers occur in similar forests but generally at lower altitudes, and Moreau (1970) considered that these were the only two migrants to penetrate this montane-forest habitat. Blackcaps also utilize gardens, thickets and broadleaved woodland in East Africa, and occur from herbaceous undergrowth to the tops of tall trees (Pearson 1978).

Blackcaps, then, live in a variety of habitats. Nevertheless, they have a distinct preference in the breeding season, on migration and in the winter for closed vegetation with some vertical structure.

3

BLACKCAP
POPULATIONS

Territory

Male Blackcaps begin to establish territories as soon as they arrive on their breeding areas. A territory can be defined as an area which is defended against members of the same species. In the case of the Blackcap, defence is also against closely related species, as will be described below. The function of territory has been the focus of much discussion. For the Blackcap, its prime function is likely to be the provision of an area where the members of a pair can obtain all of the food requirements for themselves and their young without competition from neighbours. Territory-holders will learn all the features of their areas in intimate detail, the best feeding sites at any particular time, the best places to build the nest, the best bolt-holes when faced by predators, etc. This knowledge will maximize the chances of successfully rearing offspring. A territory should be sufficiently large to meet the requirements of the Blackcap family, but not so large that it becomes energetically expensive to defend (the bigger the territory the longer the borders to admit intruders). Individual territories may vary in size according to the quality of the habitat, the quality of the male defending it, and the number of males settling in a particular habitat. Average territory size will be larger if fewer birds are competing for territories.

A territory may also act as a place where the male can attract a mate and where pair-bonding can develop in relative peace and quiet. The spacing-out of nests may also reduce the rate of predation, for, with low densities, predators will have difficulty learning the particular features of Blackcap nest sites.

Territoriality may also limit the number of pairs which are able to nest, but only if there are more birds than available habitat. This is probably not the case in many habitats in most years.

There are several ways in which Blackcaps may establish their breeding territories. Three approaches were described in a study of ringed birds in southern Germany (Barlein 1978). Some birds moved extensively around the habitat on arrival, and established a territory later. Most were first-year males, which presumably were exploring the habitat for potential territories and unfilled places. The second strategy was to occupy a large area initially, the defended area gradually shrinking over time to the size of the breeding territory. Other individuals, mainly the older birds, occupied their breeding territory directly, presumably having previously bred successfully at the site; these adults were found to settle, on average, within 120 m of their previous nesting site, 25 per cent of them occupying the same territory. Some 41 per cent of adults returned to the study area, so they showed philopatry, or fidelity to the previous breeding site. The others probably largely succumbed in the interim. Only 7.6 per cent of birds breeding for the first time returned to the study area and they settled, on average, 240 m from their birthplace. Young birds suffer much higher mortality than adults, but whether this accounts entirely for the poor rate of return is unclear. First-year birds are often less site-faithful because they are the ones which look for new opportunities for colonization.

The boundaries between territories are usually settled during song duels, males singing loudly against one another (Chapter 6). Arguments between males are then restricted largely to clearly defined discontinuities in the habitat, such as paths or edges of vegetation. Singing males become increasingly excited and eventually chase one another, sometimes for several minutes at a time. They raise their crowns and fan their tails, and sometimes fly with slow, deliberate wingbeats. On perching, they will face one another with mouths wide open and wings beating. Vigorous fights are frequent, the males sometimes grappling with one another on the ground. If territories are closely packed, several males may join in a chase, calling loudly. The boundary disputes cease when territories are stabilized, song then being the main vehicle of territorial defence, although wandering males are quickly evicted. Males are rarely aggressive towards females, and females only occasionally chase one another during territorial disputes.

Some males may be unsuccessful in attracting a mate and leave their territories in late May. By then, others have bred success-fully and desert their territories once the young have become independent. Neighbouring males then quickly enlarge their territories to encompass the vacant space. In the south German study area, territories at the end of April averaged 0.35 ha (range 0.13–0.75 ha) but had grown by the end of May to 0.51 ha

Male Blackcaps are highly aggressive at territorial boundaries.

(range 0.26–1.12 ha), an increase of 45 per cent. Those territories in the centre of the study area (average 0.92 ha) were much larger than those at the edge (0.39 ha). It may be that the shrub layer is more luxuriant at the edge of the wood, because of the additional light penetration, and this in turn results in a greater abundance of insects.

The situation in Wytham Wood, in Oxfordshire, seemed rather different from that in Germany, with territories smaller in late May than they were earlier in the season, while reductions in territory size have also been reported once the nest was completed (Raines 1945). It is possible that, in these situations, the population density was high and that new arrivals led to a contraction in territory of established birds.

In Wytham Wood, the average territory size was 0.20 ha in scrub and 0.76 ha in mature woodland, reflecting territory sizes at the edge and in the centre of the German study area described above. The territory sizes of Garden Warblers in these Wytham habitats were almost identical to those of Blackcaps (Garcia 1981).

In southern Europe, Blackcap territory sizes appear to be smaller. For example, in tall maquis in Gibraltar they averaged 0.16 ha, while in low maquis they were 0.24 ha. These scrub habitats in the south will have very high spring densities of insects.

Territories are defended areas, but one study of ringed birds in France showed that Blackcaps ranged widely outside their territories during the breeding season (Ferry *et al.* 1981). The average territory size, determined by mapping singing males, was 1.12 ha. The average home range, measured from recaptures of ringed birds, was 7.4 ha, more than six times greater than territory size. Home ranges overlapped with adjacent territories, and females had much greater ranges than males. The reasons for this were not discussed. The recent application of genetic-fingerprinting techniques to paternity studies of other species has shown, however, that monogamous relationships are often not quite what they seem, both males and females seeking extramarital relationships. Male infidelity has been known for a long time and potentially results in more offspring for the male at little cost to himself. Female infidelity is likely to result in more genetically diverse broods, at a considerable advantage in an unpredictable environment; females may also, by mating with males who are genetically superior to their mates, acquire good-quality genes in their offspring. Female infidelity is, of course, bad news for the male, because he will be unsure if the offspring he is helping to rear contain his genes. It has even been suggested that the main function of territory in birds is not to ensure a good food supply for the family, but rather to reduce the chance of the female having extramarital relationships. This, it is argued, is the reason for the decrease in territory size when the clutch is completed and the female is no longer fertile. Whether any of this occurs in the Blackcap is unknown, and further study of ringed birds is required to see if the wanderings of males, and especially of females, outside the territory is a more general phenomenon than the evidence currently suggests.

Not all birds in a population manage to hold territories. At the south German study site, the percentage of unpaired male Blackcaps was 5 per cent and 8.7 per cent over two years. It is perhaps surprising that more males do not forgo the rigours of defending a territory if the numbers of mated females seeking casual sex are as high as suggested in studies of other songbirds!

Blackcaps sometimes form territories in winter, usually when they have a good supply of berries or nectar-rich flowers to defend. Some 9 per cent of those wintering in Gibraltar returned there for a subsequent winter (Garcia 1989). In East Africa, some Blackcaps become territorial in late winter and sing regularly from specific songposts (Pearson 1978). Birds are otherwise solitary or wander in small flocks outside the breeding season, often consorting with other species such as tits, thrushes or finches.

Territoriality between species

In the previous chapter it was shown how closely related species of bird may avoid competition by living in different habitats or by exploiting different parts of the same habitat. If this does not result in sufficient separation, they may actively compete for space and hold mutually exclusive territories in the same habitat. There are a number of instances of interspecific competition between species-pairs of *Sylvia* warblers, several involving the Blackcap.

Eliot Howard, a steelmaster by profession and a director of the once famous firm Stewarts and Lloyds, was also one of our most distinguished amateur ornithologists. Many of his detailed observations were made in his native Worcestershire. *Territory in Bird Life*, published in 1920, is a milestone in ornithology. It is

When Blackcaps are caught and removed from nest territories Garden Warblers will often move in.

Blackcaps show especial aggression towards Chiffchaffs in nesting territories.

worth quoting his observations on the interactions between Blackcaps and Garden Warblers in full:

'All the Warblers are exceedingly pugnacious, the fighting being especially severe between those that are very closely related. The Blackcap and the Garden Warbler are constant rivals, and the scenes which can be witnessed when the two meet in competition are interesting from many points of view. The birds not only pursue and fight with one another, but their emotional behaviour reaches a high level of intensity – excitable outbursts of song are indulged in, tails are outspread, wings are slowly flapped, and feathers raised – in fact the attitudes assumed are similar in all respects to those which occur during the contests which are so frequent between the respective individuals of each species; and it would be difficult to point to any one item of behaviour which is not also manifest at one time or another during the battles between these rivals, and still more difficult to trace any difference in the intensity of the excitement. And if we are satisfied that the fighting in the one case is purposive, so, too, must we regard it as having some biological purpose to serve in the other. But the

Garden Warbler is not the only bird that acts as a stimulus to the instinct of the Blackcap; Whitethroats are often attacked, and the Chiffchaff is a source of irritation. Even when a male Blackcap is engaged in incubation, it will leave its nest on the approach of a Chiffchaff, and, having driven away the intruder, proceed to sing excitedly. At other times both male and female will combine to attack this small intruder.'

Raines (1945) noted that Blackcaps and Garden Warblers held mutually exclusive territories, and the same territory may be occupied by either species in successive years. In Sweden, it was suggested that Garden Warblers were dominant over Blackcaps and displaced the latter from better habitat when they arrived (Cody 1978). Somewhat different conclusions were reached in an experiment conducted in Wytham Woods, near Oxford (Garcia 1983). In the first and third years of the study, territories were mapped and it was confirmed that there was little overlap in these between the two species. In the second year, Blackcaps were lured into mist-nets by playing tape recordings of their song, and they were held in captivity until the end of the experiment. There were nine Blackcap territories in the area, but other birds moved in as territory-holders were removed, so that over the spring 23 birds were removed; nine Garden Warblers moved in, twice as many as in the first and third years of the study, and they occupied habitat normally inhabited by Blackcaps. It appeared, then, that Blackcaps were able to exclude Garden Warblers from territories and, in interspecific interactions, they are clearly dominant over Garden Warblers. Both species defend their territories effectively, but, in Wytham Woods, unestablished Blackcap males were seen to intrude into Garden Warbler territories twice as often as the converse and they rigorously chased Garden Warblers. Garden Warblers which intruded into Blackcap territories withdrew at the approach of the territory-owner (Garcia 1989). More Garden Warblers could nest in this part of Wytham Woods in the absence of Blackcaps, and there were potentially three times as many Blackcaps as actually held territories. Presumably, interactions both within and between the species were preventing establishment.

Why there should be a difference in dominance between Blackcaps and Garden Warblers in Sweden and those in England is unknown. Blackcaps are dominant over Garden Warblers in Finland, even though the latter is by far the more numerous species. It may be that the Swedish study area actually provided better Garden Warbler habitat and was initially occupied by those Blackcaps which were unable to establish territories in the optimum

Blackcap habitat. The outcome of interactions between the two species is probably very finely balanced and may depend on the quality of both the habitat and the individual birds.

Interactions between other species-pairs of *Sylvia* warblers also occur. For example, Common Whitethroats and Lesser Whitethroats often hold mutually exclusive territories. In southern Europe Marmora's and Sardinian Warblers are aggressive towards one another, as are Sardinian and Spectacled Warblers. Blackcaps and Subalpine Warblers respond vigorously to one another's songs (Cody and Walter 1976).

Why are there so many apparent interspecific interactions between *Sylvia* warblers when habitat division among the majority of songbirds is so precise? It has been suggested that it is due to environmental uncertainty, to which *Sylvia* warblers respond by potentially occupying a broad range of habitats (Cody 1978). Warbler habitat is often successional, being transitory in time but likely to be repeatable in space. This unpredictability has been increased by the activities of man, through, for example clear-felling, forest management and fire. Furthermore, as warblers are mostly long-distance migrants, there is uncertainty about the competitive regime that any one species will encounter on return to its breeding grounds. This will depend, for example, on the mortality that each species may have suffered outside the breeding season. By having the capacity to utilize a broad range of habitats, members of populations have the flexibility to select from a wider choice of sites until a territory of satisfactory quality is acquired. This may also, however, bring them into conflict with related species with similar broad habitat ranges.

Population trends

The current British population of Blackcaps is estimated at 800,000 pairs, making it the most numerous of our *Sylvia* species. There are about 500,000 pairs of Common Whitethroats, 200,000 pairs of Garden Warblers, and a mere 50,000 pairs of Lesser Whitethroats. Blackcaps can therefore be described as common, but we should put such statements into perspective. The population of our own species in Britain is almost 55 million, and the average man weighs more than 4000 times the average Blackcap, so that the biomass of *Homo sapiens* in Britain is more than 140,000 times greater than that of *Sylvia atricapilla*!

Before the massive deforestation of Britain, Blackcap populations would almost certainly have been much larger. Approximately

45

9 per cent of the land is currently forested, but well over half of this is conifer plantation, mostly monocultures of Corsican Pine and Sitka Spruce. By comparison, France has 27 per cent of its land area covered in forest and West Germany has 29 per cent. If we assume that all of England and Wales was clothed in forest before man became a significant force in landscape change, and that a density of one pair of Blackcaps per ha was typical for mature woodland, then 15 million pairs would have been supported. Primeval forest may have held lower densities, for densities in the Białowieza forest in Poland, considered to be the last untouched forest in Europe, average 3 pairs per 10 ha. There would still have been 4–5 million pairs of Blackcaps. The world population of Blackcaps is currently estimated to be of the order of 70y million birds (Berthold and Schlenker 1991).

The British Trust for Ornithology (BTO) began its Common Birds Census (CBC) in 1962 to monitor changes in the populations of our commoner breeding species. It was introduced at a time when pesticides and the intensification of agriculture were both having major impacts on wildlife. There were, however, few data with which to assess such impacts, and, without information, conservationists could exert little influence on agricultural policies. Each year some 300–400 plots are covered in the CBC, and the observer maps the positions of all birds seen and heard on his plot over a series of visits, ideally ten, during the breeding season. From the clusters of registrations, the numbers of territories of each species on each plot can be estimated. *Population Trends in British Breeding Birds* (Marchant *et al.* 1990) provides a fascinating review of the results of the first 30 years of the scheme.

During this period, the Blackcap has shown a constant trend of increase (Figure 3.1). Ringing numbers and submissions of nest record cards indicate that the increase began at least as early as the mid-1950s. This growth is also reflected in the number of Blackcaps passing through coastal bird observatories (Langslow 1978). The increase in the CBC Index has been greater on farmland than in woodland. Some 79 per cent of farmland plots were occupied in 1988 compared with 56 per cent in 1968, a rise of 23 per cent. Comparable figures of occupancy for woodland plots were 88 per cent and 71 per cent, an increase of 17 per cent. As the Blackcap is primarily a woodland breeder, it seems likely that more birds are forced to hold territories in suboptimal farmland habitats as woodlands become full.

This growth in Blackcap numbers appears to have occurred over much of Europe. There was a progressive increase in numbers

Fig. 3.1 *The Common Birds Census Index for Blackcaps on farmland, and woodland plots in Britain since 1964. Adapted from Marchant,* et al. *(1990)*

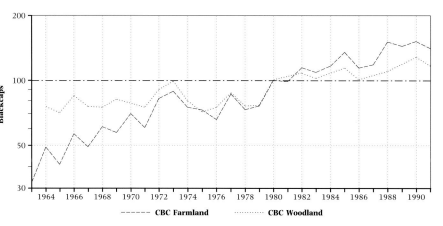

ringed in Sweden from 1960 to 1969; they stabilized in the 1970s ('Österlöf' and Stolt 1982) and have since increased again. At the ringing station of Helgoland off the North Sea coast of Germany, seven times more Blackcaps were ringed, on average, over the years 1970–79 than in the years 1953–59 (Moritz 1982). Increases have also been reported from Finland, Denmark, the Netherlands, Belgium, Germany, the former Czechoslovakia and Austria. They may not have been looked for elsewhere.

The situation of the Blackcap over the past 30 years contrasts sharply with that of the other migrant *Sylvia* warblers in Britain. Garden Warbler numbers peaked in the mid-1960s, then showed a trend of decline, reaching a low in the mid-1970s (Mason and Hussey 1984). Thereafter there has been a slow increase, but not apparently to the population levels of the early 1960s. Common Whitethroats declined drastically in numbers in 1969, when it was estimated that as many as 90 per cent of the population of 1968 may have failed to return. Numbers remained low for most of the next 15 years and have only recently shown some signs of recovery. Lesser Whitethroats have exhibited large and irregular fluctuations: for example, they were quite numerous in the early 1960s but numbers gradually fell away. In the 1980s there were also good numbers, but, at the time of writing (in early June 1993), Lesser Whitethroats have hardly put in an appearance in the woodlands and farmlands of my local patch in north-east Essex.

The huge decline in Common Whitethroat numbers in 1969 is perhaps most easy to explain. There was a sudden failure in the rains of the Sahel, the savannah region of West Africa south of the Sahara Desert, in the previous summer and autumn. The majority of Common Whitethroats winter in this area. Sedge Warblers and Redstarts were similarly, though not so severely, affected. Rainfall has fluctuated since, but has remained below the long-term average, as have numbers of Common Whitethroats. The decline in the Garden Warbler may also be linked to the Sahelian drought, although that species declined later and recovered earlier than the Common Whitethroat. Garden Warblers winter much further south in Africa than Common Whitethroats, but it may have been difficulties in crossing the drought-affected Sahara and sub-Saharan zone, rather than difficulties in the winter quarters, that caused its decline. There may, of course, be other reasons about which we know nothing. Lesser Whitethroats migrate south eastwards, entering Africa through the eastern Mediterranean, so they are not influenced by conditions in West Africa. They are, however, on the edge of their range in Britain, and such populations are known to experience irregular fluctuations.

It is more difficult to explain the steady increase in Blackcap numbers. It could be argued that they are taking advantage of a shortage of Garden Warblers, for it was shown earlier that these two species may compete for territories. The increase in Blackcaps, however, began before the decline in Garden Warblers, and Garden Warblers have been able to re-establish their population in the face of further increases in Blackcaps, even though the latter species is known to be competitively dominant. It has been suggested that the success of Blackcaps is due to the fact that the majority winter around the Mediterranean and are hence unaffected by events in West Africa (Lack 1989). This could explain why Blackcaps have not declined but not why they have continued to increase, unless they are occupying habitat vacated by less fortunate congeners, for which, as I have suggested above, there is no evidence. Furthermore, it has been shown recently that annual *changes* in the numbers of Blackcaps on farmland closely mirror those of both Common Whitethroat and Sedge Warbler, even though Blackcaps are increasing (Bibby 1992). As numbers of both Sedge Warbler and Common Whitethroat are closely correlated with Sahelian rainfall, it is suggested that more Blackcaps than hitherto believed winter in the Sahel, or that they are affected by weather patterns that are correlated with rainfall there; or there may be another factor which has not been considered. Quite frankly, we have no firm idea why Blackcap populations are increasing, but a possible reason is proposed below.

Mortality

Despite this increasing population, Blackcaps do, like all small birds, suffer a very high mortality. From ringing data in West Germany, the annual death rate has been estimated at 68 per cent for first-year birds and 54 per cent for adults (Berthold 1978). This high mortality among young birds is typical, for they are inexperienced and hence more likely to fall victim to accidents, predators or food shortages. Older birds learn to cope with potentially life-threatening situations. This high average juvenile mortality means that changes in the breeding population from year to year are more likely to be influenced by the survival rate of the young than by that of the adults.

Other estimates of annual Blackcap mortality are 40 per cent (all ages) from Belgium and 58 per cent for adults in Gibraltar (Fouarge 1981b; Finlayson 1992). The oldest known Blackcap from the British ringing scheme was almost seven years old, while an individual of eight years has been recorded elsewhere.

There are many causes of death, but they can be grouped into a number of categories: starvation, weather, accidents, disease, natural predation, and being killed by man. Determining the relative significance of these mortality agents is important to the ornithologist and conservationist, but it is also extremely difficult, especially in the case of small migratory birds like Blackcaps. The causes of mortality are usually determined from ringing returns, but these are subject to a number of biases. Birds which starve to death, are taken by predators or fail to complete a long sea-crossing are highly unlikely to be found, whereas ringed birds which crash into windows or are shot by hunters have a much greater chance of being reported.

From the British ringing scheme, the proportions of birds dying of various causes have been estimated (Hickling 1983). Some 12.5 per cent were traffic victims, 2.5 per cent died from collisions, 10 per cent were killed by cats and 3.9 per cent by other predators, 27.5 per cent were killed or deliberately taken by man, and the remaining 43.5 per cent died from unknown causes. In a study of birds ringed in Belgium, more than 50 per cent of recoveries involved individuals shot or trapped, mostly in the Mediterranean area (Fouarge 1981b).

The biases become obvious, I think, from the above percentages. More than half of the deaths appear to be due to the activities of man, directly or indirectly, and his pets. For example, many millions of birds are undoubtedly killed by traffic each year, and this cause of death has almost certainly increased over the last 40 years with the exponential growth in vehicle numbers. For some species this factor may be more important than is realized, for some of the best hedges for nesting sites run alongside roads. However, there has been no systematic survey of traffic casualties since the early 1960s, when only two Blackcaps were recorded on almost 250 miles (400 km) of road surveyed at regular intervals during the year (Hodson and Snow 1965). By contrast, 43 Common Whitethroats, a hedgerow-nester, were found killed by traffic in the survey. The ringing scheme clearly overestimates the role of traffic in the mortality of Blackcaps because such a small proportion of the population nests alongside roads.

Similarly, the 2.5 per cent killed by collisions, largely crashing into windows, is likely to be an exaggeration. In the late autumn of 1976, however, there was a spate of such deaths in north-east Scotland (Macdonald 1978).

Pesticides have had a major impact on many bird populations and, as described above, were one of the major reasons for initiating the Common Birds Census. There is no information on the effects of pesticides or other contaminants on Blackcaps, and the latter are unlikely to encounter significant amounts in their breeding haunts. In parts of Africa, however, large quantities of pesticides are used, some of which have long been banned in Europe, but it is not known whether Blackcaps come into contact with them. There is evidence from Sweden that Africa is a significant source of pesticides in some migrant passerines, since DDT levels in Common Whitethroats declined during the summer breeding season, although they were never initially high enough to reduce breeding success (Persson 1972).

Of avian predators on the breeding grounds, Sparrowhawks are likely to be the most significant, more so now that their population is expanding rapidly following the steep decline in the 1950s and 1960s caused by pesticides. Nevertheless in a study in southern Scotland, where admittedly Blackcaps are scarce, they made up only 0.02 per cent of the Sparrowhawk's prey (Newton 1986). Eleonora's Falcon is a predator of migrants crossing the Mediterranean, and it times its breeding season so that it has young in the nest in autumn, when migrants are most abundant. No doubt some Blackcaps fall victim to it, but, as the falcon is so scarce and the migratory bird population so large, the impact on numbers will be negligible. Gulls have been shown to be significant predators of thrushes and Starlings as tired migrants fly the last few kilometres low across the North Sea to a landfall in East Anglia

The domestic cat is a major predator of Blackcaps and other small birds.

(Macdonald and Mason 1973), and it is a depressing experience to see them knocked into the water or caught in flight when they are within sight of the safety of land. Smaller birds such as Blackcaps probably run similar risks at times, but I am not aware that it has been observed.

Magpies and Jays are likely to be significant predators on eggs and young, as are mammals such as Weasels, Stoats and squirrels (Chapter 5). Domestic cats, however, are probably the most important predators of Blackcaps. The ringing data indicate that 10 per cent of all Blackcaps are the victims of cats. This may be an exaggeration, for cats often bring prey back to the house, while ringers may operate ringing stations in their gardens and keep cats as pets! Conversely, many cat-owners feel guilty about the depredations of their pets and may be disinclined to report ringed victims. In Britain most of the woodlands are small and are close to habitations, so cats range freely in Blackcap habitats. The role of cats as predators has been assessed when considering the impact of a steadily increasing Magpie population on songbirds. It was estimated that, where Magpie populations were densest, the average territory of around 5 ha would have 25 cats in suburban areas and 74 cats in urban areas. The cats would kill around 400–600 birds per Magpie territory annually, set against which the Magpie predation was insignificant (Birkhead 1991).

Finally, we can turn to human predation. The slaughter of vast numbers of migrants in the Mediterranean region merely for pleasure continues to bring shame to us all. On the tiny island of

Malta alone, up to three million birds are shot annually, several million more being trapped, or caught on those despicable limed twigs (Fenech 1992). Some of the traditional methods of trapping birds are barbaric. In the Mediterranean area, it has recently been estimated that up to 1000 million birds die at the hands of man each year (Magnin 1991), or approximately 20 per cent of the total flying south each autumn. This agrees rather well with the figure estimated from ringing returns, of 27.5 per cent of Blackcaps being killed by man, or in excess of 24 million Blackcaps each year.

The killing of Blackcaps appears to be especially intensive in Portugal, Spain, Italy, Greece, Algeria and Morocco (McCulloch *et al.* 1992). However, it is extremely difficult to determine whether such pressure is reducing breeding populations of migrants, for losses through hunting may be compensated for by reduced natural mortality (but *see* below). Clearly, the Blackcap, with increasing populations, can withstand these losses, but the species is neither a major nor any longer a legal quarry species in most countries where it is killed. Hunting may have a much greater impact on major quarry species which are also under pressure from other factors. Surely, at the end of the twentieth century, it is wrong to consider our wildlife merely as an exploitable resource. Blackcaps, and indeed all other migrants, are not an essential source of protein for the Mediterranean peoples – at best a small proportion of Black-caps may end up in jars as pickled delicacies. There has to be an ethical dimension to our attitude to wildlife – our wild birds have a right to share the planet with us. I have shown that there are many factors causing mortality of Blackcaps. A majority of these operate independently of the number of Blackcaps present; for example, a violent storm during migration over the sea may kill a large proportion of birds irrespective of the number present. However, there may be mortality factors which are density-dependent, killing a greater proportion of the population as population density increases. Density-dependent factors are important because they operate to regulate the population, keeping it within close limits around a mean number. They lead to population stability and hence the optimum use of resources. The relative significance of density-independent and density-dependent factors in controlling populations has been a controversial area of ecology for over 40 years and, for the majority of species, the importance of density-dependent mortality is still largely unknown, for the detailed, long-term life-history data required to demonstrate it are just not available.

A recent attempt at examining population limitation in Blackcaps has been made with BTO data using key factor analysis, a technique which itself has been controversial (Baillie and Peach 1992). The results showed that the key-factor, that factor causing most deaths, in Blackcap populations was the mortality outside the breeding season. This is hardly surprising, since that period encompasses the majority of the year and includes mortality from fledging and through the summer, when a large number of inexperienced birds enter the population and find fending for themselves difficult. It also includes losses on both migrations and through the winter period. This mortality was found to be only slightly density-dependent, and no other mortality factor (loss of eggs, loss of young, etc.) capable of regulating the population was detected. One might not expect such regulatory mortality in a population which has been consistently increasing over more than three decades, but maybe, too, these data sets were not the most suitable for detecting regulation.

Earlier, I suggested that we have no idea why Blackcap numbers are increasing. Blackcaps undoubtedly still suffer heavy losses in the Mediterranean region at the hands of man, but the species became protected throughout the EC under the Birds Directive of 1979. There is some evidence of a decrease in Blackcap hunting intensity over the last four decades (McCulloch *et al.* 1992), with more hunting directed at legal quarry species, such as the larger thrushes. In particular, trapping and liming may be declining as Mediterranean countries become more affluent. The Blackcap may be especially vulnerable to hunting since a substantial proportion of the population winters in the Mediterranean, whereas most trans-Saharan migrants are exposed for only a few weeks when large numbers of many species pass through the area, helping to swamp the impact of hunters. Any decline in such pressures may therefore benefit Blackcaps especially.

4

BREEDING BIOLOGY

Spring arrival

The earliest spring migrants to Britain, arriving in March, are Chiffchaffs, Sand Martins and Wheatears. The Blackcap is included in the second wave of arrivals, generally appearing in the first week of April, along with Swallows, Willow Warblers and Yellow Wagtails. The other *Sylvia* warblers put in their first appearance in mid-April, with a third wave of migrant species.

The pattern of earliest arrival dates of *Sylvia* warblers in Leicestershire over 50 years is shown in Figure 4.1, taken from the annual reports and files of the Leicestershire and Rutland Ornithological Society. The few March dates for Blackcap almost certainly include some records of overwintering birds, the earliest arrivals being mainly in the first half of April. The first Garden Warblers are mostly in mid-April, but there seem to be three peaks in arrival dates. Common Whitethroats first appear in mid-to-late April, while Lesser Whitethroats show a similar pattern but with a distinct peak in the five days beginning 21 April. The mean arrival dates for the species in Leicestershire are:

Blackcap	8 April
Common Whitethroat	19 April
Lesser Whitethroat	23 April
Garden Warbler	24 April

From the Eure-et-Loir département of France, west of Paris, a long series of dates showed the same order of arrival as above, but, not surprisingly, warblers appeared earlier, two weeks in the case of Blackcaps and one week in the case of Common Whitethroats and Garden Warblers (Labitte 1955). Average arrival dates in central Sweden, Finland and north-west Russia are in mid-May (Cramp 1992).

The bulk of birds, of course, arrive rather later than these harbingers. The main immigration of Blackcaps into Britain takes place in late April and early May, with most individuals of the other

Figure 4.1 *Percentage of first-arrival dates, in five-day periods, of* Sylvia *warblers in Leicestershire over a fifty-year period, 1942–91*

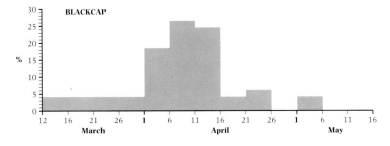

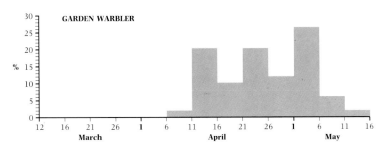

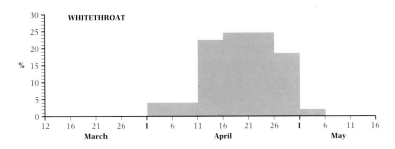

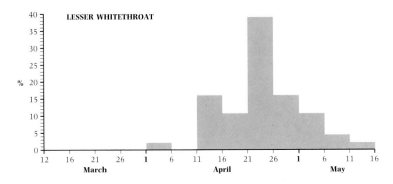

Fig. 4.2 *Arrival dates of Blackcaps in Leicestershire, 1942–91, plotted as a five-year moving average (on the vertical axis, 20 = March 20, 40 = April 9, etc. The shaded areas represent periods when the arrivals fall outside the 95 per cent confidence limits of the mean. Note that arrivals were particularly late in the 1950s and early 1960s, and have been especially early since the mid-1970s. The trend towards earlier arrivals is statistically highly significant.*

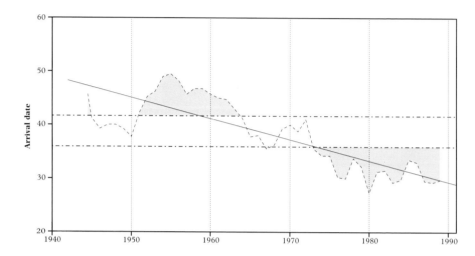

Sylvia species arriving later in May (Riddiford and Findley 1981). Male Blackcaps tend to arrive earlier than females (Davis 1967) and first-year males later than adults (Barlein 1978). In Germany, the arrival of a colour-ringed population took place over a period of at least 24 days.

I have also examined the arrival dates of Blackcaps in Leicestershire over time (Figure 4.2), and it is quite clear that Blackcaps are now occurring significantly earlier than they did in the 1940s and 1950s. By contrast, Garden Warblers and Common Whitethroats, two trans-Saharan migrants, are arriving slightly (but significantly) later, while there is no overall trend in the arrival dates of Lesser Whitethroat, a species migrating from the south-east.

What is the reason for this earlier trend in Blackcap arrivals? It might be argued that it merely reflects the greatly increased interest in birdwatching, with more observers looking for early birds. As the trend is absent in other *Sylvia* warblers, however, this argument can be dismissed. With the increase in wintering Blackcaps, it may be that these are mistaken for early migrants. While this undoubtedly accounts for some March records, most wintering Blackcaps in Leicestershire occur in gardens, whereas most records of arrivals are of singing males in breeding habitat. I therefore believe that it is a genuine trend of earlier arrival. This view is supported by the fact that Blackcaps are laying earlier now than they used to (Humphrey Crick, pers. comm.). Their breeding population has also increased steadily over the last three decades (Chapter 3). Natural selection may be operating to favour earlier arrivals, which obtain the best territories in an increasingly crowded environment and therefore leave more surviving young. Such a hypothesis needs testing but certainly the first birds to arrive in my local wood are always to be found in the same places, suggesting that the very best territories may be limited in number.

These early arrivals may not, however, be unique to the last part of the twentieth century. In the first part of the nineteenth century, the poet John Clare wrote, of *The March Nightingale*:

> *The while the Blackcap doth his ears assail*
> *With a rich and such an early song*
> *He stops his own and thinks the nightingale*
> *Hath of her monthly reckoning counted wrong.*

That the Blackcap seems generally to have been called the March Nightingale, at least in Clare's native Northamptonshire, suggests that it was widespread in that month. We should perhaps be talking about late arrivals in the 1940s and 1950s, rather than early arrivals in the 1970s and 1980s. In view of my suggestions at the end of the last chapter, it may be worth pointing out that in Clare's day guns were both less accurate of aim and in many fewer hands than they are in this century; and, while, no doubt, Mediterranean peoples trapped and limed birds, their own populations would have been much smaller than today. Hunting pressure may therefore have been less intense. There may also, of course, be the possible influence of long-term fluctuations in climate.

Courtship

Blackcaps first breed when they are one year old. Once settled in a territory, the male needs to attract a mate. Blackcaps are largely monogamous. Bigamy has been recorded (Barlein 1978), and there was also a case of two males assisting a female in feeding young (Harper 1986). Song plays a major part in attracting females (Chapter 6), but the male also builds simple nests (cock nests) soon after arrival which he shows to prospective mates. Cock nests are generally built close to songposts, and up to seven such nests may be built before the female finally accepts one, which she indicates by adding nesting material to it on her first visit (Raines 1945). The male lures the female to his nest by displaying.

During courtship the male flies excitedly from tree to tree, singing loudly, and he may fly towards the female in a butterfly-flight. The black crown feathers are raised and lowered, the wings drooped or gently beaten, and the back feathers ruffled. Mating takes place usually in the early morning (Howard 1907–14), and after the first mating the intensity of courtship declines. As the male approaches, the female crouches with drooped wings, which are shivered just before copulation. The male's nest-showing behaviour may also stimulate the female, who then crouches nearby with open bill until the male leaves the nest to copulate with her (Siefke 1962).

The nest

The cock nest takes one or two days to build and, if it is accepted by the female, completion takes place over an additional two to five days, most building occurring in the early morning. The nest is a tidy structure of roots, tendrils, grasses and the stems of herbs, with the rim covered in wool and cobwebs. It is lined with finer material, including hair. One nest in Germany was lined with

Table 4.1 *Percentages of* Sylvia *nests found in different types of vegetation (from Mason 1976).*

	Blackcap	Garden Warbler	Whitethroat	Lesser Whitethroat
Bramble	47.8	52.8	32.0	47.1
Nettle	8.5	10.9	18.4	1.2
Hawthorn	7.3	4.0	7.9	21.3
Blackthorn	2.5	1.3	2.3	8.1
Elder	5.6	1.6	0.3	0.6
Rose	3.6	7.5	2.7	9.9
Grasses	0.3	2.4	13.7	0
Gorse	0.6	0.2	2.6	0.6
Other sites	23.8	19.3	20.1	11.2
Total vegetation types used	49	63	90	26
Total nests	914	623	3799	333

Fig. 4.3 *Distribution of nest heights of the* Sylvia *warblers. From Mason (1976)*

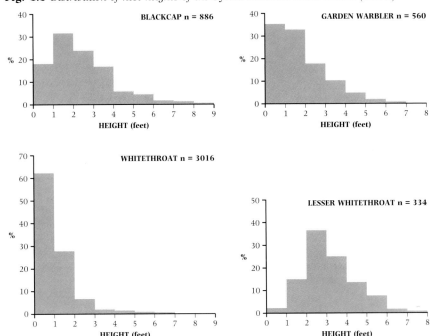

180 horse hairs of 15–40 cm in length (Deckert 1955). In one case, a female used an old nest of a 'Long-tailed Tit as a source of nesting material. The nest is suspended by basket handles.' (Keen 1989) Nests are some 5.5 cm high, with a cup depth of 2.7–4.5 cm; their external diameter averages 10 cm and the internal diameter 6 cm (Deckert 1955; La Mantia 1982).

The main nest sites of the *Sylvia* warblers, determined from an analysis of nest record cards of the BTO, are given in Table 4.1. Bramble was the most frequently utilized site for all species, although Common Whitethroat used it significantly less often than the other species. Blackcap nests were found significantly more often in Elder than were those of the other warblers, while nests of Lesser Whitethroats occurred significantly more often in Hawthorn and Blackthorn. A greater proportion of Common Whitethroat nests was located in Nettles, grasses and Gorse. These differences in nest site presumably reflect differences in choice of habitat (Chapter 2), with Blackcap and Garden Warbler being primarily birds of deciduous woodland, where bramble is often a major component of the ground vegetation. Lesser Whitethroats are strongly associated with overgrown hedgerows, which are often dominated by Hawthorn and Blackthorn, and Common Whitethroats are more birds of scrub and wasteland places.

In other parts of Europe, bramble is much less significant as a nest site. In Finland spruce and Juniper are very important to *Sylvia* warblers, and in south Germany spruce, Nettles and bramble. *Sylvia* nests found in Bird Cherry in south Germany are almost certainly those of Blackcaps, while nests found in pine are most likely to belong to Lesser Whitethroats (Barlein *et al.* 1980).

The height at which nests were placed in Britain is shown in Figure 4.3. Although there is considerable overlap, there is a general trend from highest to lowest in the sequence Lesser Whitethroat, Blackcap, Garden Warbler and Common Whitethroat. This same trend in nest heights of the four species has also been found in Finland and Germany (Haartman 1969; Barlein *et al.* 1980). There is also a general trend of declining average nest height from south to north across the breeding range of Blackcaps, while in Germany nest heights increase with increasing altitude.

Thus, although there is considerable overlap, there is ecological separation in the siting of nests in respect of both vegetation type and nest height.

Breeding seasons

The reproductive strategies of birds have evolved to produce the maximum number of surviving offspring, which can be achieved by optimizing both the timing of the breeding season and the number of eggs laid. If too few eggs are laid the parents will leave few surviving offspring, whereas if too many eggs are laid the young may starve or leave the nest underweight, thus lowering their chances of surviving to breed themselves. Similarly, birds laying too early or too late in the breeding season may have their young in the nest when food for them is in short supply. Reproduction involves costs as well as benefits and natural selection operates to produce a reproductive strategy which maximizes benefits in relation to costs.

Reproduction is energetically costly, especially for the female. Resident birds can build up their fat reserves steadily, and courtship-feeding of the female by the male assists in accelerating her energy gain prior to egg-laying. Blackcaps, however, are not known to courtship-feed. Migrant birds will arrive on their breeding grounds depleted of fat reserves, which have to be regained quickly, and on arrival they must also establish territories and find mates. There is some recent evidence to suggest that this results in migrants laying later compared with residents with respect to the date of peak clutch size. That is to say that, with resident passerines, clutch size over the whole breeding season rises to a peak and then declines, whereas with migrants the peak clutch size coincides with the start of the breeding season (Crick *et al.* 1993a). This again emphasizes that migrant warblers mostly begin breeding as quickly as possible after arrival, so that their young hatch when food is most available. Clutch sizes are discussed further below.

Blackcaps begin laying some three weeks after the first arrival of the females. According to data from the BTO nest record cards, the breeding seasons (i.e., the start of egg-laying) of the four migrant *Sylvia* warblers in Britain are as shown in Figure 4.4. Breeding seasons extend from April to July for Blackcap and Lesser Whitethroat, from April to August for Common Whitethroat and from May to July for Garden Warbler. There are always exceptions, and a Blackcap's nest containing a single egg was found in Norfolk on 11 March 1845 (Morris 1860). In all species, however, most clutches are started in May, the peak being slightly earlier in Blackcap and slightly later for Garden Warbler. The Garden Warbler has a much more sharply defined breeding season than the other species. This may be because it arrives later and has to begin its nesting activities quickly so that its eggs hatch during the period of greatest abundance of food, as described above.

Figure 4.4 shows the generalized breeding seasons summarized from many years of data, but breeding seasons show considerable annual variation. The range of mean laying dates between years was 14 days for Blackcap, 15 days for Garden Warbler and 17 days for the two whitethroats (Mason 1976). Variations in breeding season are influenced both by the date of arrival and by local conditions, and species tend to vary in parallel in their laying dates. However, there are long-term trends in breeding seasons which must reflect trends of climatic change. In the 1950s and 1960s, the Blackcap's average laying date was 16 May. By 1978 this had been delayed to 24 May, but since then it has steadily been brought forward, being 18 May by 1990. Of 82 species analysed by the BTO, 33 have exhibited a recent trend towards earlier laying dates, 23 showing a hump-backed curve similar to that shown by the Blackcap, with later breeding during the mid-1970s (Crick *et al.* 1993b).

The breeding seasons of *Sylvia* warblers in Germany are very similar to those in Britain, but, in Finland, peak egg-laying does not occur until June (Barlein *et al.* 1980; Gnielka 1987). A tropical

Fig. 4.4 *The laying dates of* Sylvia *warblers, shown as percentage of clutches started in each five-day period. From Mason (1976)*

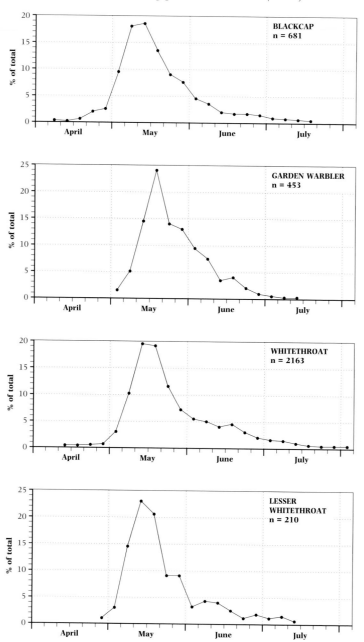

population of Blackcaps on the Cape Verde Islands breeds mainly from the end of August to the end of November, with a second, smaller, breeding season from mid-January to the end of March (de Naurois and Bergier 1986; Berthold 1988). These are presumably adaptations to two periods of rainfall, a major one in autumn and a much smaller one in late winter.

Breeding seasons of birds may be extended because individuals will lay a repeat clutch if they lose their first. They may also rear a second, or indeed several, broods once the first has become independent. The nest-record-card analysis indicated that only a small proportion of *Sylvia* warblers were double-brooded, but the method of data collection might tend to underestimate these. In a study of a colour-ringed population of Blackcaps in south Germany (Barlein 1978), repeat clutches averaged 34 per cent, with a gap of 12 days between the loss of the first brood and the start of the repeat clutch. The percentage of successful birds laying a second clutch was 5 per cent in one year and 13 per cent in the next, there being a gap of three weeks between fledging the first brood and starting the second clutch. This interval is exactly the same as that between the initial arrival of females and the laying of the first egg, and it must represent the time required to gain condition and put on fat for the development of the eggs. Only a small proportion of Common Whitethroats is double-brooded (Diesselhorst 1968), and two broods are infrequent in Lesser Whitethroats and exceptional in Garden Warblers. Second broods are therefore not the rule in *Sylvia* warblers.

When replacing a clutch of eggs, or starting a second clutch, Blackcaps almost always build a new nest. They use the same territory, but new nests are, on average, built some 28 m from the original.

Eggs

The eggs are generally light buff in colour, mottled with light brown and grey, with a few spots and streaks of dark brown. They are occasionally white and unmarked, while an erythristic type has also been reported with a pinkish ground colour and red markings. They average 19.7 mm long and 14.7 mm in diameter.

The clutch size of Blackcaps ranges from two to seven eggs. The distribution of clutch sizes of the *Sylvia* warblers, determined from nest record cards, is shown in Figure 4.5. In all species a clutch size of five is the most frequent but clutches of four are almost as common in the Garden Warbler. The overall mean clutch sizes were:

Blackcap	4.65
Garden Warbler	4.44
Whitethroat	4.67
Lesser Whitethroat	4.79

This order of clutch sizes seems to be the general rule in Europe, with Lesser Whitethroats having the largest clutches, followed by Common Whitethroat, Blackcap and Garden Warbler. For all the species, there is a tendency for larger clutches to be laid further north. This could be a response to the longer period of daylight, allowing more food to be collected for the nestlings, or possibly to the shorter potential breeding season, reducing the possibility of re-layings and second broods. In southern Germany, Blackcaps laid the largest clutches in wet deciduous forest, the optimal habitat, and the smallest clutches in marginal wasteland (Barlein *et al.* 1980). Blackcaps lay fewer eggs, on average, on Corsica than on

Fig. 4.5 *Clutch sizes of the* Sylvia *warblers* (from Mason 1976)

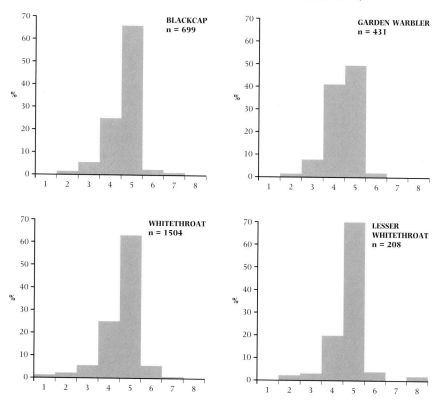

Fig. 4.6 *Mean clutch size (± two standard errors) of Blackcaps through the breeding season. Adapted from Mason (1976)*

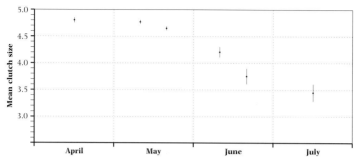

the mainland (Piacentini and Thibault 1991): smaller clutches are the general rule in populations of birds on temperate islands, and it is suggested that this is due to the milder, less fluctuating temperatures on islands compared with those on the mainland.

The clutch sizes of all four *Sylvia* warblers, and indeed of many other species, decline as the breeding season progresses. In the Blackcap, the average to the middle of May is 4.7 eggs, but it then begins to decrease, reaching a minimum of 3.5 eggs in the few clutches laid in July (Figure 4.6). This is presumably an evolutionary response to the seasonal decline in food supplies, for parents would have difficulty in providing sufficient food for a large brood towards the end of the breeding season.

Incubation of the eggs begins with the penultimate one laid (Gnielka 1987) and takes, on average, 11 days (range 10–16 days), the same incubation period being reported for other *Sylvia* warblers (Mason 1976). Both sexes incubate the eggs, but only the female does so at night.

Nestlings

The nestlings all hatch within a day of each other. They are initially naked and pink, with pink bill and feet. The mouth is red, with the gape lemon-yellow or white. By the time they fledge the bill and legs are greyish.

Both parents assist the young in hatching, remove the eggshells and feed their offspring, sharing nest duties and nest sanitation. There are, however, a few instances where the male has taken over the duties of rearing the first brood while the female incubates a second clutch. The young are brooded normally by both sexes at

65

As they grow older nestlings call noisily for food on the arrival of the parent.

first, but only at night (by the female) as they grow. They begin to call for food when about six days old and become very noisy at eight or nine days old. Nestlings which hatch later develop more quickly than those in earlier broods. Interestingly, Garden Warblers, with their later arrival and more synchronized breeding, develop more quickly than Blackcaps, again presumably an evolutionary response to the period of maximum food availability. This accelerated development appears to start in the egg.

The young Blackcaps generally leave the nest when 11 or 12 days old, before they are able to fly, and stay close by for the next few days. They begin their first attempts at feeding when 12–14 days old. The family stays together for two to three weeks after the young have fledged.

Nest protection

Both eggs and young are vulnerable to predation. The brooding parent tends to sit quietly and tight on hearing the alarm calls of its mate. Similarly, young nestlings will crouch in the bottom of

These noisy nestlings are growing their primary wing feathers and the nest is beginning to look decidedly too small for them.

the nest when alarmed, but when larger they will burst from the nest ('explode') prematurely when disturbed by a likely predator. Male Blackcaps chase other bird species away from the nest site when they have young, and will also mob predators, both parents sometimes combining in an attack. The parents also perform distraction displays, moving with half-open wings and flirting tail, sometimes half-running, half-flying, along the ground. Such displays are generally silent, although snatches of low-intensity song may be given.

ABOVE *Fledglings leave the nest before they are able to fly and are only fed by the parent for two to three weeks as they learn the skills of foraging for themselves.*

BELOW *With drooping wings and flirting tail, the male will distract a predator away from the nest.*

Productivity

Despite the care and attention of the parents, many eggs and young are lost both to predators and through the effects of adverse weather. Late-spring thunderstorms are especially damaging to nests of small birds. In Britain, 55 per cent of those Blackcap nests which failed were robbed by predators and 36 per cent were deserted, often because of the effects of weather (although causes of failure are poorly documented on nest record cards). Predation was also a major cause of failure in other *Sylvia* warblers, being especially so for the Lesser Whitethroat (74 per cent of all failures). Nest predators are rarely observed but will include Magpies, Jays and Carrion Crows among the birds, as well as mammals such as rats, squirrels, Stoats and Weasels. Blackcaps are also occasional hosts to Cuckoos, especially in central Europe, and the degree of egg-mimicry is said to be generally good (Wyllie 1981).

Blackcaps are sometimes parasitized by Cuckoos, especially in Central Europe.

Table 4.2 *Overall breeding success of* Sylvia *warblers*

	Number of eggs laid	% eggs hatched	% young fledged	Young fledged as % of eggs laid
Blackcap	2484	75.6	79.9	60.4
Garden Warbler	1419	71.9	80.1	57.6
Common Whitethroat	4034	68.9	85.0	58.6
Lesser Whitethroat	791	77.7	83.4	65.0

The breeding success of the *Sylvia* warblers in Britain is summarized in Table 4.2. The hatching success of Blackcap eggs was 76 per cent and 80 per cent of eggs which hatched produced fledged young. The corresponding figures in East Germany were 93 per cent and 92 per cent, and in Italy 65 per cent and 75 per cent. Garden Warblers and Common Whitethroats in Britain had a somewhat lower hatching success but more Common Whitethroat young fledged. Overall, a greater proportion of Lesser Whitethroat eggs resulted in fledged young, with Garden Warbler eggs being least successful.

Some 62 per cent of Blackcap nests in Britain produced at least one fledged young compared with 41–46 per cent in Continental studies (Barlein *et al.* 1980; Gnielka 1987; Lambertini 1981; Mason 1976). In Britain, clutches laid in May produced more fledged young, on average, than those started in other months, so individual nest success is greatest for those clutches started during the main laying period.

Overall success rates are generally similar in other *Sylvia warblers*, although Garden Warblers were less successful, only 55 per cent of nests producing fledged young. Garden Warblers had a smaller clutch size, a more synchronized laying period and a lower overall

Table 4.3 *Percentages of nests producing at least one fledged young in years of low and high population (adapted from Mason 1976).*

	Per cent success	
	Low-population years	High-population years
Blackcap	73.3	63.9
Garden Warbler	71.1	50.4
Common Whitethroat	70.1	61.6
Lesser Whitethroat	53.7	61.3

success rate, all of which are probably due to their later arrival on the breeding grounds, so that food supplies may already be waning when the majority of young are in the nest.

Success rate is also lower for all species, except Lesser Whitethroat, in years when populations are high (Table 4.3). It may be that predators find nests easier to locate in years when there are more nests. This has been demonstrated directly with that well-studied species the Great Tit (Gosler, 1993), where more nests are raided by Weasels as the density of the tit population increases. That the Lesser Whitethroat does not fit into this pattern may be due to the fact that, even in years of high population, it is not especially numerous.

The productivity of nests is defined as the proportion of clutches which reach fledging multiplied by the mean number of young per nest which reached the fledging stage. The productivity for all *Sylvia* species peaks in May. The overall productivity for the breeding season was determined, from nest record cards, as follows:

Blackcap	2.5
Common Whitethroat	2.8
Lesser Whitethroat	2.7
Garden Warbler	2.1

Thus, the two whitethroats had the highest overall productivity.

5

DIETS AND FORAGING

Blackcaps are omnivores, taking a wide variety of invertebrates and fruits, but diet changes markedly with the seasons. During the breeding season insects are the predominant food, but, following the moult, Blackcaps become largely frugivorous through late summer, autumn and winter. Experiments with captive birds have shown that this shift in dietary preference is controlled by an internal biological rhythm (Berthold 1976a, b).

The Blackcap can be described as a 'gleaner', carefully searching among foliage and twigs for edible items. Individuals will occasionally hover in front of vegetation to pick off food, a technique used much more frequently by leaf warblers and Goldcrests. They may sometimes hunt like flycatchers to take passing insects. They also feed on the ground.

Birds which spend large amounts of time searching for food items tend to have broad diets: anything found that is edible will be eaten. Such species are known as 'generalists'. All of the *Sylvia* warblers can be so described.

Spring diets

When they arrive at their breeding grounds in April, Blackcaps take many berries of Ivy as well as insects. Berries may form an important food if the spring is late and cold. Pollen and nectar may also be taken in spring. On migration through the Camargue, southern France, Blackcaps have been found contaminated with *Citrus* pollen which adhered to their beaks and foreheads as they sipped nectar from the flowers (Ash *et al.* 1961). They have been observed to tear corollas of *Hibiscus* to reach nectar. Other nectar sources have included *Eucalyptus*, Goat Willow, Maple and Dogwood, and the birds can act as pollinators for this last species (Calvario *et al.* 1989).

Sixteen orders of insects, comprising at least 78 families, have been recorded as food. Blackcaps also take spiders, harvestmen, ticks, false scorpions, centipedes, millipedes, woodlice, earthworms and snails (Cramp 1992). Small snails are swallowed whole and provide a rich source of calcium for developing eggs.

In a wood near Oxford, the diet of Blackcaps has been determined by analysing their droppings (Garcia 1981). More than 75 per cent of their diet consisted of bugs (Hemiptera), with aphids being especially important early in the breeding season. Diptera (mainly craneflies), beetles and caterpillars made up most of the remainder of the diet. In Denmark, Blackcaps on migration took a varied diet of insects, woodlice and snails from April to mid-May (Laursen 1978), with birds foraging from ground level to the treetops. From mid-May most of the prey consisted of slow-moving insects, such as moth larvae and planthoppers, caught in the canopy as the leaves unfurled. Other studies have shown that beetles, especially weevils, may comprise up to half the spring diet.

Young in the nest are fed mainly on soft-bodied insects, especially caterpillars and craneflies. Beetles become more important as the young grow and caterpillar populations decline from June onwards. Snails and grit are also provided for additional calcium for growth. Nestlings are occasionally fed berries, especially of Ivy, but probably only when insect food is scarce. Soft fruits, such as currants and strawberries, are sometimes given, possibly as a source of water.

The *Sylvia* warblers all have a diverse diet, and individual habitat patches may support several species of warbler. Habitat selection and the evidence for mutually exclusive territories between species, to avoid competition for food, have already been described (p. 21). Another way of reducing direct competition is to forage in different parts of the same general habitat. The classic study on niche separation was carried out in eastern North America on five species of the New World wood-warbler, which were found to spend much of their time hunting in different parts of spruce trees (MacArthur 1958). Do *Sylvia* warblers show similar separation?

The foraging heights of five *Sylvia* species at a study site in Sweden are shown in Figure 5.1. In general, the foraging patterns reflected the overall vegetation structure in the preferred sub-habitats of the warblers. Blackcaps, however, foraged higher in the taller vegetation, whereas Garden Warblers and Lesser Whitethroats foraged at lower heights in the same vegetation.

Foraging heights have also been studied in Sardinia (Cody and Walter 1976). Again, there was considerable overlap between species. Both Blackcaps and Subalpine Warblers are canopy feeders. Where both occurred together in Evergreen Oak woodland, the Blackcap had a narrow feeding range in the upper canopy, but in one study area, where the Subalpine Warbler was absent, the

JPPW

Blackcaps regularly drink and bathe and are frequent visitors to ponds and bird baths in gardens.

Blackcap had a broader range of foraging heights, and fed, on average, lower in the canopy. These species are highly interactive in territorial encounters. Sardinian Warblers were mainly canopy feeders in the absence of other *Sylvia* species, but in oak woodland, where both Blackcaps and Subalpine Warblers were also present, the species was restricted to the low scrub of the understorey.

In contrast to these studies, Blackcaps and Garden Warblers did not differ significantly in their average foraging height and diet in an Oxfordshire woodland (Garcia 1981). There was also no difference in the diet between the two species on spring migration in Denmark. Differences in foraging heights probably have only a limited role in keeping *Sylvia* warblers ecologically separate during the breeding season.

In Sweden Sylvia warblers forage at different height in their breeding habitat (p. 73 and Fig. 5.1): Blackcap; Lesser Whitethroat; Garden Warbler; Barred Warbler and Common Whitethroat.

Fig. 5.1 *Percentage of time warblers spent foraging at different heights in a Swedish study site. The study area consisted of a patchy habitat of Juniper and rose heath, interspersed with a low woodland of oak and poplar. Adapted from Cody (1978)*

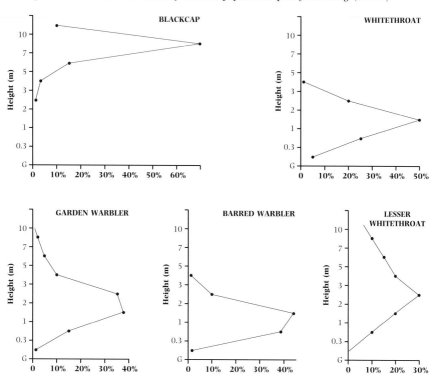

The switch to fruit

Blackcaps become increasingly frugivorous from July, at a time when many fruits start ripening and many insects, especially the large, juicy larvae, decline in numbers. In Switzerland, the sizes of insects taken by Blackcaps were found to decrease steadily from August to October, aphids making up the majority of the animal food in late September and October (Turrian and Jenni 1991).

In addition to availability, there is also a biological reason for the switch to fruit. Insects are rich in proteins, an excellent food source for young nestlings and for making new feathers during moult. However, insects are generally low in carbohydrates. By contrast, fruits are full of concentrated sugar which is very efficiently assimilated and converted to fat, enabling birds to put on weight quickly prior to migration. Aphids may have similar properties, for, feeding directly on the phloem of plants, they are also rich in sugars. Some insects must always be included in the diet in order to supply the protein needs for long-term body maintenance.

Blackcaps are, of course, predators when feeding on invertebrates. Fruit is generally swallowed whole, the seed within passing intact through the gut, a process taking as little as 12 minutes for individual berries, although the digestion of a whole meal takes over two hours (Groebbels 1932). The quick passage of the fruit through the gut enables rapid processing of the pulp. By excreting seeds, which survive to germinate, Blackcaps act as seed-dispersers. By contrast, species such as Bullfinch and Hawfinch, which are interested in the seed primarily as food, are seed predators.

The Blackcap's vegetarian diet is as diverse as is its carnivorous one, with more than 70 taxa recorded as being eaten (Cramp 1992); they take what is available. In their studies of frugivory in the Chiltern Hills of southern England, Snow and Snow (1988) recorded 23 species of berry being taken by Blackcaps, most observations of feeding involving Ivy (23 per cent of the total) and Elder (20 per cent). Holly, Woody Nightshade, Spindle, White Bryony, Perfoliate Honeysuckle and Privet each made up 5–10 per cent of the total feeding observations, the use of other species being much scarcer. Feeding on blackberry was surprisingly infrequent in this study. Blackcaps were observed feeding on fruits in all months, but there were few records from March, June and November. Frugivory was most marked from July to September, making up 52 per cent of the total observations. Holly berries were taken mainly in January and February, Ivy in April and May and Elder in August and September.

The Snows observed that most fruits were plucked while the birds were perched, but very occasionally they would fly out to take a fruit or would cling to a fruit with fluttering wings until it was pulled free from the plant. Blackcaps often fed in small groups, frequently with other species. They took a meal consisting of 5–10 per cent of their body weight, then retired for periods of 10-20 minutes before taking further meals.

Mature sand dunes are clothed in a scrub of berry-bearing species, and frugivory has been studied at such a site in Lincolnshire, on the east coast of England, where migrant warblers often congregate (Boddy 1991). Here, Blackcaps were found to prefer the berries of Woody Nightshade over blackberries in July and early August. Garden Warblers showed a similar but less marked preference, whereas Common Whitethroats and Lesser Whitethroats preferred blackberries to fruits of Woody

Nightshade. Elder berries were extensively eaten by Garden Warblers and the two whitethroat species as soon as they ripened in mid-August, but Blackcaps came to feed on them later, preferring blackberries in mid-August. It was estimated that the faeces of Blackcaps contained 75 per cent fruit in July and August, the proportion increasing to 90 per cent in October, when Elder berries were the main fruits taken. In November, fruits of Elder and Sea Buckthorn predominated, with four other species taken in lesser amounts.

Boddy estimated that, on migration in September, a Blackcap could obtain 75–90 per cent of its daily energy requirement from Elder berries in less than 10 per cent of the available feeding time. Some 20 per cent of the diet was consistently non-fruit, mainly insects, which presumably provided nutritional requirements, especially protein, not available from an exclusively fruit diet. Blackcaps in autumn in Spain also take a small proportion of insects in a diet mainly of fruit (Jordano 1988).

Mistletoe is rather scarce in Britain and is an insignificant component of Blackcap diets, but in Lorraine and Anjou, respectively in eastern and west-central France, the berries are extensively eaten (Heim de Balsac and Mayaud 1930). In Lorraine, Blackcaps took Mistletoe berries in March and April, following their return from wintering areas. In Anjou, where Blackcaps winter, Mistletoe berries were exclusively taken in severe winters and bird densities were high where berries were abundant. Individuals defended groups of plants against other Blackcaps. Blackcaps take the Mistletoe fruits and place them on a branch to squeeze out the seed; the fruit is then eaten, and the seed left. Blackcaps were considered to be the principal seed-dispersers because Mistle Thrushes, the other main feeders on Mistletoe, swallowed berries whole and scattered seeds haphazardly in their faeces, the majority landing in sites unsuitable for germination.

In the Mediterranean region, Blackcaps are almost exclusively frugivorous on migration and in winter. Many Mediterranean fruits have a higher nutritive value than those of northern Europe, with a greater average protein and fat content overall, making them better winter foods. The fruits of the Lentisc (Mastic Tree) and Olive contain 16 per cent and 42 per cent fat, respectively. Fruits also contain a lot of water, which is often very scarce in Mediterranean shrublands in late summer. A positive water balance is essential for

Hillside macchia by a stream in Andalucía in September. This fruit-rich habitat supports large numbers of migrant and wintering Blackcaps.

onward migration. Up to 21 species of fruit were recorded in Blackcap diets in one study in Spain (Jordano and Herrera 1981), with eight species in a single faecal sample. The most frequently taken fruits were from Lentisc, Olive and Strawberry Tree, with Madder, *Osyris* (a broom-like species) and a climber, *Smilax aspera*, taken infrequently but consistently.

In the scrublands (*macchia*) of Spain, Herrera (1984) estimated a fruit density of 100,000 per ha in November and December. Although fruits of various species differ widely in their proportions of pulp, size of seed and nutritive value, they are remarkably uniform in overall size, with a diameter of 5–10 mm. The dominant seed-dispersers were Blackcaps, Sardinian Warblers, Robins and Blackbirds, and these removed 89–100 per cent of the crop of fruits smaller than their gape width. Larger fruits were poorly dispersed. Blackcaps took some 60 per cent of their fruit diet from the Lentisc, which was both the most nutritious fruit in the study area, in terms of fat and protein, and often the most abundant. Herrera considered that Blackcaps were the main dispersers of Lentisc seeds and Lentisc fruits were, in turn, the major source of the birds' energy. However, Blackcaps also took small amounts of fruit from scarce species, and these tended to be richer in trace elements than the major fruits, thus helping to provide a balanced diet (Jordano 1988).

In another Spanish study (Jordano 1982), Blackcaps were the most important dispersers of the seeds of Southern Blackberry, taking 30 per cent of the seed crop. It was estimated that, on an average day, some 32,400 seeds from a parent clone were removed by birds, about 9700 of these by Blackcaps!

Seasonality in the main fruits taken by Blackcaps has been described from Croatia (Tutman 1969). Figs were taken almost exclusively in September and October, Bay Laurel fruits were eaten from late November or December, and Olives in late winter. Commercial Olive crops, and indeed wild fruits, vary in abundance depending on climate. In some years a large proportion of olives are left on trees because the crop is poor, they ripen late and they are unprofitable to harvest. In such years the fruiting of wild species is poor, and large numbers of Blackcaps feed in Olive orchards (Rodriguez de los Santos *et al.* 1986). Blackcaps are often nomadic in their southern wintering areas, and the selection of habitat depends upon local availability of fruits. Fruit choice depends upon availability, but Blackcaps show preferences for fruits yielding high energy (Jordano 1988). In addition to fruits, flowers of Dwarf Furze were eaten in winter in Spain, while in Gibraltar the nectar of aloes, a plant introduced from South Africa, is extensively fed upon in January and February when native fruit stocks are depleted (Finlayson 1992).

Those populations of Blackcaps which winter south of the Sahara also eat a diet largely of fruits, supplemented with insects (Snow and Snow 1988; Cramp 1992).

Garden Blackcaps

Increasing numbers of Blackcaps are wintering in the British Isles (p. 18) and a considerable proportion frequents gardens. When the BTO's Garden Bird Feeding Survey was initiated in the winter of 1970/71 no Blackcaps were recorded, but they increased steadily during the 1970s and were taking food at almost 16 per cent of feeding stations by the end of the decade and at more than 30 per cent by 1982 (Glue 1982; Hickling 1983). Blackcaps are most frequent in the gardens of south-west England, and are much more regular visitors to suburban than to urban gardens. They are in thirty-fourth place in the league of birdtable-visitors. By contrast, a more recent, preliminary study has shown that, in southern Europe (Spain, Portugal and Italy), the Blackcap is the ninth most frequent garden-visitor (Thompson 1990).

During a special survey of wintering Blackcaps in 1978/79 (Leach 1981), the food taken was observed on 2879 occasions (Table 5.1). Bread and fat were the most frequently taken items. One bird fed exclusively on Christmas cake throughout the winter! (Hickling 1983). Twenty-two types of berry were eaten, with *Cotoneaster* most often recorded (41 per cent of total berries taken), followed by Honeysuckle (16 per cent), Ivy (7 per cent) and *Berberis* (5 per cent). Feeding on the nectar of Winter Jasmine has

Apples are important for Blackcaps feeding in gardens in winter.

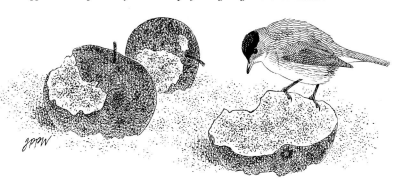

Fruit is a major component of the diet of Blackcaps from late summer and they will feed on apples provided for them.

also been observed (Hardy 1978). Blackcaps have also learned to feed on peanuts in feeders. Such behaviour was unrecorded before the 1970s but there were 158 records in the special survey. Initially, the birds hovered in front of feeders and took peanuts, but they soon learned to cling briefly, like some Robins do. Other Blackcaps became as agile as tits.

At feeding stations, Blackcaps are very aggressive both to conspecifics and to other species. In aggressive encounters between the sexes, the two were equally likely to emerge dominant. Most interspecific aggression is directed at tits, finches and Dunnocks,

In their Mediterranean winter quarters Blackcaps feed extensively on the fruits of olive and they will also take nectar from flowers of Citrus trees.

Even Blackbirds may be driven from birdtables by Blackcaps.

but birds as large as Starlings and Blackbirds may be driven from birdtables. Blackcaps may also be bold towards man: individuals took a variety of foods from the hand outside the galley of an army camp in Algeria (Linsell 1949).

Clearly, Blackcaps are adaptable and opportunistic feeders, and this has enabled them increasingly to exploit winter birdtables.

Table 5.1 *Frequency of foods taken in winter by Blackcaps in Gardens (adapted from Leach 1981)*

Food item	percentage	Food item	percentage
Bread	21.1	Seed	6.6
Fat	20.3	Cooked potato	2.6
Berries	15.5	Cheese	2.4
Apples	13.6	Porridge	2.1
Peanuts	9.7	Other foods	6.1

6

BLACKCAP LANGUAGE

Communication between animals is conducted by acoustical, visual, tactile and chemical signals, and sometimes even by using electricity. With birds, visual and sound signalling are especially prominent. The various displays of Blackcaps have already been described but they are quite modest compared with those of other bird species, whereas vocal communication is highly developed. There are a number of special advantages of oral communication for small birds living in dense vegetation. Sounds travel quickly over considerable distances and are not obliterated by obstacles, so that a message can be received and understood without the caller being observed. They are extremely economical, for a small effort can produce a large response over a wide area. For example, a warning call may keep an intruder out of a territory without the need for chasing or fighting. There is also a wide spectrum of sounds available for use.

The utterances of birds can be considered as a form of language, because they communicate information between individuals. We can divide the vocalizations of Blackcaps into two groups; song and call notes. The song is used for the establishment and defence of the territory, to attract a mate and to maintain the pair-bond. The call notes are concerned with co-ordinating the activities of members of the group, such as responses to predators or maintaining contact.

Song

The Blackcap's song imparts several pieces of information. It identifies the species, Blackcap, and that the individual is a male. It warns that he holds a territory in a specific location and that he will defend it against other males. It also signals his presence to females.

Morris (1860) wrote of the song 'A very beautiful roundelay is that of the Blackcap, inferior only in the estimation of many to that of the Nightingale. Its tones, though desultory, are very rich, deep, full, loud, varied, sweetly wild and witching'. The full song,

Fig. 6.1 *Seasonal variation in the frequency of Blackcap songs recorded during hour-long transects through a wood in north-east Essex*

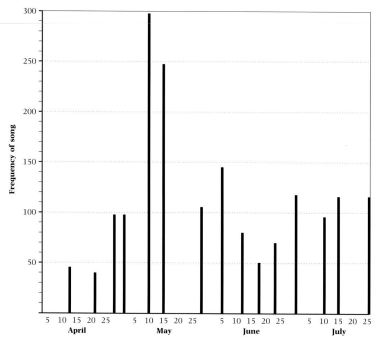

which may last up to half a minute, begins with a rich, varied warbling, bursting into a loud final soprano flourish which can be heard over a considerable distance. Songs are given in quick succession, with one or two seconds between, in bouts of 2.5 minutes. Blackcaps will sing for long periods, in one case for more than three hours (Simms 1985).

There is a distinctive variant of the song known as the *Leiern*, a series of fluting notes, which was first described from the Alps but has since been heard further north and west, as well as in Iberia. The ending of the Leiern song recalls the typical song of the Great Tit. I heard this variant uttered by a Blackcap in a small wood in north-east Essex in 1994, the first occasion that I have recorded it in Britain. All this bird's songs ended in a loud 'teacher, teacher'. It was still singing distinctly two weeks later, while the only other male in this wood sang the typical phrases of a British Blackcap.

In the winter quarters in East Africa, song is heard from late January and with increasing intensity into March, when the birds depart (Pearson 1978). The frequency of song through the breeding season is shown in Figure 6.1. During 1993, transects lasting one hour, and finishing always before 7 a.m., were made in Stour Wood, north-east Essex, at approximately weekly intervals. Song was first heard on 12 April. It reached a peak in the middle of May, when Blackcaps were pitching their songs against one another, so-called song-duelling. Such song is especially loud and rich, with emphasis on the fluting terminal flourish. Towards the end of May, the amount of song had declined considerably and no song-duelling was heard. At this time the most persistent songsters were in places where there had been none before. Perhaps they were Blackcaps which shifted territory after failing to attract a mate, or they may have been late arrivals to the wood. There was some resurgence of song in early June and an increase in song-duelling. A violent storm on 2 June may have washed out nests and forced Blackcaps to lay a replacement clutch. Song then fell back again, and by 24 June only a single bird was singing vigorously. Song and song-duelling increased again in July, probably indicating the laying of second clutches of eggs by some birds.

In July, the dawn chorus consisted mainly of Blackcaps, Chiffchaffs and Wrens against a backcloth of the cooings of Woodpigeons, whose song is particularly intense at this time. Blackcap song was not heard in Stour Wood after 28 July, and my last singing bird of the year was in Kent on 2 August. Chiffchaffs also abruptly ceased singing at the end of July. Unlike Chiffchaffs and Willow Warblers, Blackcaps appear not to sing on

Males song-duelling at territory boundary.

Fig. 6.2 *Diurnal variation in the frequency of Blackcap songs recorded during hour-long transects through a wood in north-east Essex on 7 May 1993*

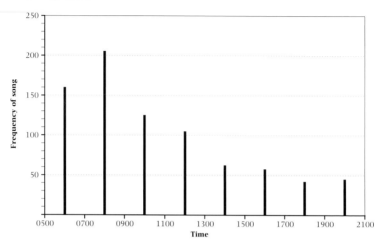

migration, although I once heard song from one in a mixed group of warblers on 17 August.

I also attempted to record the seasonal pattern of singing of other *Sylvia* warblers in Stour Wood, but, although they were present, their song was intermittent after May. They were all at low density and did not have contiguous territories, so that, once they had paired, there may have been little incentive to sing. Last songs were heard from Garden Warbler on 15 July, from Lesser Whitethroat on 16 July, and from Common Whitethroat on 18 July.

The intensity of Blackcap song varies through the day (Figure 6.2). On 7 May, 1993, the same transect as described above was walked at two-hourly intervals, again for one hour, and all songs were noted. Blackcaps began singing some 15 minutes before official sunrise, some 30 minutes after Song Thrush, Blackbird and Robin. These last three generally break off to feed at about the time Blackcaps begin singing. Song activity peaked between 7 a.m. and 9 a.m. and then fell steadily, so that, by the afternoon, the amount of song was only about 25 per cent of that at the peak. There was no increase in activity towards dark.

Blackcaps sing mainly from cover, but they will sometimes use an exposed perch, especially early in the season, and they occasionally sing in flight. There is considerable variation among individual songsters, and this can be detected by the human ear. There may also be geographical variation, although this has not been formally analysed using a sound spectrogram.

Once Blackcaps are mated, the song may deteriorate, and those singing towards the end of the season have a rather broken song, as if their musical abilities are disintegrating. When courting a female, the male sings a fast, continuous, excited chatter, without the terminal flourish. There is also a subsong, which has been described as prolonged and rambling, although to my ear it is quite attractive, and several other variants are recorded (Cramp 1992). Subsong has also been heard from females.

The Blackcap's song is easily confused with that of the Garden Warbler and many birdwatchers have great difficulty in differentiating them. Garden Warbler song lacks the terminal flourish of the Blackcap's and is generally more sustained, mellower and quieter, but with a faster tempo. With practice the two can generally be distinguished, but the problem is made more difficult because Blackcaps often mimic Garden Warblers. Indeed, the Blackcap is an accomplished mimic and, as early as 1860, Morris listed imitations of Nightingale, Blackbird, Song Thrush and Robin, as well as Garden Warbler. Since then, a number of other species have been added to the list, including Willow Warbler, Lesser Spotted Woodpecker and Wryneck. Warblers and thrushes are most likely to be mimicked.

In addition to this similarity between the songs of Blackcap and Garden Warbler, Blackcap song is said to be easily confused with that of Subalpine Warbler on the island of Sardinia. Here, Sardinian, Dartford and Subalpine Warblers are also easily confused, especially the last two (Cody and Walter 1976). Blackcaps closely approached a tape recorder playing Subalpine Warbler song. A vagrant Icterine Warbler (a member of a different warbler genus), singing one May day in Kent, caused both a Blackcap and a Common Whitethroat to sing vigorously and chase the intruder, even though its song bore no resemblance to that of the Blackcap and only a little to that of the Common Whitethroat (Gilbert 1986).

Why are these *Sylvia* songs so similar when most songbirds can be readily distinguished by their songs? Cody and Walter (1976) suggested that it is a case of character convergence: the songs have become similar so that species respond to one another, this promoting interactions between the species and thereby segregating territories, as described in Chapter 3. An alternative view is that they are similar because of the dense nature of the

Although subdued in plumage, the male Blackcap has a righ melodic song.

vegetation in which the warblers live (Garcia 1989): the character-istics of the song enable it to penetrate thick undergrowth and thus be heard at some distance.

Call notes

The commonest call is a distinctive, sharp 'tac-tac', like two pebbles being struck together. It is much harder than the similar call of Garden Warbler, which can be rendered as 'check-check'. The call of the Lesser Whitethroat is somewhat intermediate and most easily confused with the Blackcap's. The 'tac' note is used both as an alarm and as a warning when defending resources such as fruiting bushes; when excited, the calls are run together as a series of harsh notes. Blackcaps also have a mewing call, and this may be combined with the 'tac', the resulting 'mew-tac' being characteristic of groups of birds feeding on fruiting trees in winter in Spain (Garcia 1989).

Blackcaps also utter a churring note, similar to that of Garden Warbler and rather typical of the scrub warblers in general, but it is used much less often than by these other species. As well as the 'tac-tac', Blackcaps have several other alarm calls. A squealing note, rather slurred, has been heard, while a Wigeon-like whistle was heard from a bird alarmed by a squirrel. A quiet, drawn-out 'chu-chu-chu' signals the presence of a hawk, and this is also used by the female as she approaches her nestlings. Contact notes between the members of a pair include gurgling sounds and a subdued greeting call. The distress call, given for example when Blackcaps are handled, is a repeated screech. Nestlings have a series of soft cries.

7

KEEPING IN TRIM

The feathers of birds enable them both to fly and to keep warm, while their colour assists in advertisement or camouflage. There are three main types of feathers: contour feathers, down feathers, and hair-like filoplumes. The contour feathers are arranged in regular rows and give the body its general shape. The smaller down feathers lie between and beneath the contour feathers, while the filoplumes are scattered over the body between the contour feathers. Feathers are made of keratin, a fibrous sulphur-containing protein, and are very strong.

To maintain their function, feathers need regular care, and birds spend a lot of time preening. Blackcaps bathe in shallow water and can frequently be seen at garden ponds or birdbaths, especially when on migration in late summer. They have also been observed foliage-bathing during or following rain showers: the birds bathe by brushing their heads, wings and bodies vigorously against the leafy branches of various shrubs (Glue 1985). I observed similar behaviour by a juvenile Blackcap in mid-August 1993. The bird flew down to our lawn and began rubbing its belly and wings from side to side in the dew, then rubbing and flicking its tail; it preened the wetness into its plumage. It flew into an apple tree when disturbed by a Woodpigeon, but then returned and foliage-bathed for a further minute, before flying into a Portuguese Laurel to feed on berries.

Although strong, feathers do eventually become abraded and worn and have to be replaced.

Moult

Moult can be defined as the periodic replacement of the plumage, involving the pushing-out of the old feathers by the developing new ones. The growing of a new set of feathers requires a considerable amount of energy, for feathers make up 5–10 per cent of the total weight of a small bird, which therefore tends to moult at a time when food supplies are abundant and when temperatures are warm, for insulation is poorer when feathers are not fully

A male Blackcap foliage-bathing.

grown. Moult also has to be fitted in between other energy-demanding activities, such as breeding and migration.

The most common pattern of moult is the symmetrical loss of a few feathers on each side of the body, so that feather loss and gain are balanced and body function is maintained. Generally, the primary feathers of the wings are moulted in sequence, followed by the secondaries and tail feathers, and then by the feathers of the body.

The warblers show a great variety of moulting patterns, more so than in any other family of passerines. Some species have a complete moult at the end of the breeding season (post-nuptial moult), and there is no further moult until this is repeated in 12 months' time. Others have a complete post-nuptial moult, but then show a partial moult of body feathers and some wing and tail feathers in their winter quarters prior to spring migration back to their breeding areas. Still other species start the moult following breeding but this is interrupted during migration, to be completed on arrival in their winter quarters. Others have a complete moult in the wintering area.

Blackcaps moult mainly on their breeding grounds, through August and September, before they begin migration. In contrast,

93

The aviaries at 'Vogelwarte Radolfzell', Germany, where large numbers of Blackcaps and other migrants are reared.

Garden Warblers have a complete moult in their winter quarters, although some individuals may complete a wing moult before migrating (Gladwin 1969). Most Common Whitethroats begin their moult before migration, but those individuals which start late will suspend moult during migration. In general, the post-nuptial moult is delayed only in those populations which have to migrate long distances to southern Africa. There are two advantages of this strategy for long-distance migrants (Pearson 1973). First, their flight feathers will be in a fresh condition for the spring migration, which is more rapid and demanding than the autumn migration. Second there is more time available for moult in the winter quarters, and it appears to be a more leisurely affair. Thus, moulting Garden Warblers in Uganda had an average of 1.8 primaries per wing in growth at any one time, whereas Blackcaps and Whitethroats, moulting in southern Britain, had respectively 3.5 and 3.6 primaries in growth.

The adult post-nuptial moult by the Blackcap begins with the innermost primary, from early July to mid-August, and is completed with primaries 9 and 10 from mid-August to late September. The primary wing moult lasts about 50 days for birds moulting early, but is shortened by five days in those starting later. Body and tail moult is usually completed by mid-August. There may be a partial pre-breeding moult from December to March but this is often suppressed, especially in birds in the north of the wintering range. Blackcaps wintering in East Africa and summering in Scandinavia and Russia show a partial moult – again, those birds with the greatest distances to cover to the breeding grounds ensure that their plumage is in tiptop condition.

The juvenile plumage lasts only until the first autumn moult, for the loosely structured and small contour feathers, which are inadequate for insulation against the cold or for sustained flight, must be replaced, while some unfeathered areas of the body, such as the belly, require covering. The post-juvenile moult is only partial in the Blackcap and lasts longer than the adult moult, taking some 52–106 days. Blackcaps remain in their natal plumage for some two to three weeks before beginning post-juvenile moult, whereas Garden Warblers, Common Whitethroats and Lesser Whitethroats begin moulting as soon as natal growth is completed. Thus in north-east England, the post-natal moult of the Blackcap begins in the second half of July, whereas in other *Sylvia* warblers it begins in the first half of July (Norman 1990). This again reflects migration strategy. A study of the moult of hand-raised individuals of eleven *Sylvia* species showed that the earlier a species starts its migration, and the further it travels, the earlier and shorter is the moult: thus, moult in Garden Warblers lasts 30 days, while in Marmora's Warbler it is 124 days, the Blackcap being intermediate (Berthold 1988a). An exception to this general rule is the moult of the Blackcap population living on the Cape

Fig. 7.1 *Time course of post-juvenile moult in hand-raised Blackcaps. Populations are from southern Finland (SFi), south Germany (SG), southern France (SFr) and the Canary Islands (CI). Also shown is the moult of hybrids (SG X CI) from south German and Canary Islands parents. The bars indicate the duration of moult. Adapted from Berthold and Querner (1982)*

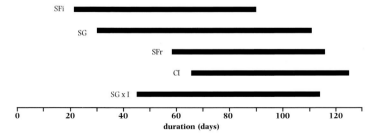

Verde Islands, which takes only 44 days; it may be that, because these birds breed twice in a year and there is an intervening dry period, there is a strong selection pressure in favour of a short moult.

The temporal pattern of the moult varies in intensity in relation to migratory habit (Berthold 1988a). The Blackcap intensifies its moult slowly towards the middle of the moulting period and then reduces it slowly, producing an intensity curve which follows a normal distribution. By contrast, the much more migratory Garden Warbler reaches the maximum intensity of moult in the first quarter of the moulting period, the intensity curve being strongly skewed to the right.

The sequence of post-juvenile moult begins with the dorsal and ventral areas, followed by the head feathers and wing-coverts and, lastly, the tail-coverts. Those Blackcaps which hatch later show significantly less replacement of the greater wing-coverts, presumably because they need to journey south before the entire post-juvenile moult is completed (Herremans 1991).

The genetical basis of moult in Blackcaps has been determined in cross-breeding experiments (Berthold and Querner 1982). Nestlings originating from populations in southern Finland, southern Germany, southern France and Tenerife in the Canary Islands were initially hand-raised in identical conditions in Germany. There was a progressively later onset of juvenile moult from the highly migratory Finnish birds through to the sedentary Canary Islands individuals (Figure 7.1). The Canary Islands and German birds were then used for cross-breeding experiments, and the hybrid offspring showed an intermediate time course of post-juvenile moult, which differed significantly from that of the Canary Islands birds in terms of onset, duration and termination.

The onset of moult in birds is triggered by changes in day length and controlled by hormones in a way which is still very imperfectly understood. There appears to be an interaction between the activity of the thyroid gland and the cycle of the gonads, the influence of the sex hormones being suppressed by the general background metabolism, which is determined by the thyroid hormone. Male and female sex hormones (androgens and oestrogens) appear to inhibit moult, because the moulting process begins as sexual activity wanes. Non-breeding or unsuccessful birds moult earlier. The injection of sex hormones into moulting birds will halt the process. Nevertheless, there is not a direct link between sex hormones and moult, because castrated birds will moult on schedule.

The photoperiod can also accelerate the development of juveniles born late in the breeding season to prepare them for migration. In Blackcaps hatched in August, the growth of the plumage, including the wing and tail feathers, the development of the second generation of feathers, and the juvenile moult started at an earlier age and were of shorter duration than in Blackcaps hatched some 72 days earlier, in May. Because of this acceleration, late-hatched Blackcaps developed migratory activity only 18 days later than those which hatched early (Berthold 1988b).

The factors influencing the pattern of replacement of feathers are also poorly understood. It may be that each feather follicle has a different sensitivity to the hormones that trigger moult, so that those feathers with the greatest sensitivity will drop first.

Weight

Birds are warm-blooded animals (homeotherms) and require considerable amounts of energy to maintain their body temperature. They are also very active creatures and use substantial amounts of energy in carrying out their daily activities. This energy has to be obtained from food. Small birds require more food per gram of body weight to stay alive than do large birds, because of their greater surface-to-volume ratio. Birds will put on weight to help them survive periods of food shortage or to prepare them for energetically expensive activities such as breeding or migration. They therefore exhibit diurnal, short-term and seasonal variations in body weight. Fat is the most efficient material to store, because it yields twice as much energy and water per gram metabolized as does either carbohydrate or protein. The water is especially valuable during migration as it prevents dehydration. Fat is stored at various sites under the skin, in the muscles and in the peritoneal cavity.

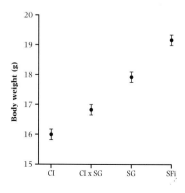

Fig. 7.2 *The pre-migratory body weights of Blackcaps. Populations are from the Canary Islands (CI), south Germany (SG), southern Finland (SFi), and first-generation hybrids (CI X SG) from Canary Islands and south German parents. Adapted from Berthold and Querner (1982)*

Fig. 7.3 *Average weights (g) of Blackcaps in ten-day periods at Wicken Fen, Cambridgeshire. Adapted from Langslow (1976)*

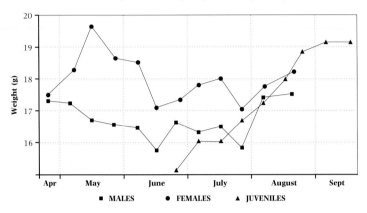

For Blackcaps. it has been shown that the determination of body weight is under genetic control (Figure 7.2). Non-migratory populations of Canary Islands birds (held in captivity in south Germany) had the lowest body weights, while highly migratory Finnish Blackcaps had the highest pre-migratory weight, south German birds being intermediate both in migration distance and in body weight. First-generation hybrids between Canary Islands and south German Blackcaps had pre-migratory body weights intermediate between those of their parents.

The average weight of Blackcaps in England and Wales during the spring is 17.5 g. They are lightest in the early morning and heaviest in the late afternoon, with a strong increase during the day, reflecting both the consumption of food and the subsequent deposition of fat. This diurnal weight change is a feature of both summer and winter (Turrian and Jenni 1991, Ioale and Benvenuti 1982). Weight losses during the night, when the bird is metabolizing but, of course, has no opportunity to feed, are of the order of 1.5–2 g. The amount of weight put on during the day in winter is directly related to the diurnal temperature change: the greater the variation in temperature, the larger the change in weight (Cuadrado *et al.* 1989).

Figure 7.3 shows typical seasonal weight changes in Blackcaps over the spring and summer period. The birds arrived at this breeding site in Cambridgeshire with an average weight of 17.3 g, but the females then rapidly increased in weight to a maximum of 19.6 g in mid-May, at a time when they were laying their first clutches. Weight then decreased, but increased again in mid-July, which probably reflected the laying of second clutches. Males lost weight during the breeding season. Both males and females put on a little weight at the end of the breeding season, although there was no evidence of pre-migratory fattening at this inland site. The juveniles put on weight steadily from late June, and at least some juveniles showed pre-migratory fattening.

Blackcaps weigh more during the moult than they do immediately before and after (Norman 1990). This may be because they require increased energy reserves to combat heat loss as feather insulation is less effective during the moult. They may also have an increased water content at this time.

Birds put on weight prior to migration, but the amount of weight gain will depend to some extent on the distance covered between stopovers. Blackcaps on migration in southern Germany put on sufficient weight to allow them to fly a further 200 km on average, but it is considered that average nightly flights are shorter than this. Interestingly, Garden Warblers, typical long-distance migrants, had similar potential flight ranges so that both species appear to cross continental Europe in short stages (Kaiser 1992). In southern Sweden, the fattest 25 per cent of Blackcaps have sufficient energy reserves to cross Europe to the Mediterranean coast without refuelling (Ellegren and Fransson 1992), but they almost certainly migrate in a series of nocturnal hops. If food is readily available, it is undoubtedly a good idea to put on additional fat as an insurance against the unexpected on migration.

Elder berries enable Blackcaps to gain weight rapidly while on migration.

Blackcaps arriving at British bird observatories in autumn have highly variable weights, this probably due to their having different origins or departure weights. Those arriving at the Shetland observatory of Fair Isle are on average some 2 g lighter than those arriving further south, presumably because they have flown further. On average, birds in autumn are about 2 g heavier than the spring weight of 17.3 g. Blackcaps may spend several days at coastal sites, putting on weight on a fruit diet. At Spurn Bird Observatory in Humberside, their average weight gain was 0.7 g per day and they were capable of putting on 1 g per day. Because they lose weight (1.5–2 g) during the night, they must eat sufficient food to put on 3 g of fat per day to achieve this weight gain. Blackcaps can build up fat reserves equal to 30–50 per cent of their body weight in fewer than ten days (Langslow 1976). The average weight of Blackcaps prior to departure was considered to be 24 g. It has been estimated that the weight loss of migrating Blackcaps is 0.15–0.19 g per hour, and, depending on departure and arrival weights, estimated flight times are 18–60 hours. The minimum flight times from the Netherlands and West Germany, from where many of our east-coast Blackcaps set off, are estimated at 11 hours and 22 hours respectively, agreeing well with the estimated flight times from weights.

In southern Spain, during the autumn migration, some 17.5 per cent of Blackcaps weighed more than 21 g and it was considered that these represent long-distance migrants, crossing the Sahara (Rodriguez 1985). The remainder probably winter in the Mediterranean.

Blackcaps wintering in Britain are subjected to colder conditions and longer nights than those wintering in the traditional Mediterranean sites. They therefore tend to be heavier, average weights being greater than 20 g over the period, with females consistently heavier than males. Blackcaps in Spain were up to 2.9 g lighter, similar to summer weights, and females weighed more than males only in the coldest months of January and February. Indeed, there is a significant latitudinal trend in winter weights across Europe, birds in central Europe being on average more than 2 g heavier than those in the Mediterranean basin (Cuadrado *et al.* 1989).

In southern Spain, the average fat value of the Blackcap falls from October to November, the former month's data including birds moving further south and still putting on migratory fat. There is then a slight but steady increase in weight from December to February, with a marked increase in March and April. In this area of Spain, there were also differences in average weights between years, which appeared to be related to the fruit crop (Cuadrado *et al.* 1989). Thus, in 1981–82, when the Olive crop was substantial, both fat content and weight of Blackcaps were significantly higher than in the following winter, when the Olive crop was poor, and in subsequent winters when the entire crop was harvested.

Blackcaps leave the Mediterranean for their breeding grounds in March and April, after putting on considerable weight, assisted by an abundant supply of insect food. The average weight of birds on Gibraltar in April is more than 20 g, and 35 per cent of birds weigh more than 21 g at this time, compared with 2.5 per cent in December (Langslow 1979). Indeed, some individuals may weigh up to 31.5 g (Finlayson 1981). In southern Spain, there appear to be two peaks in spring weights, one at 22 g and a smaller peak at 25 g, with a range of 18–29 g (Rodriguez 1985). Blackcaps at Lake Ichkeul, Tunisia in March averaged 20.5 g, with a range of 16.3–25.2 g (Wood 1982). These contrast with birds at a Saharan oasis in Morocco, where the average weight was 14.1 g and the lowest 11.3 g, little more than a third of the weight of the fattest bird on Gibraltar (Ash 1969). These Moroccan Blackcaps must have both exhausted their fat reserves and suffered dehydration as they crossed the desert.

In the Mediterranean, male Blackcaps fatten before females and leave earlier. A Blackcap leaving southern Spain at a weight of 24 g would be capable of reaching southern England in about 40 hours, having lost 6–8 g in weight. Similarly, the heaviest birds in Tunisia would be capable of reaching the south of their probable breeding range in southern Germany in one continuous flight of 36 hours, covering some 1150 km. Birds weighing 20 g would have little difficulty crossing to the northern shore of the Mediterranean, some 800 km in distance, while landfalls in Sardinia, Italy and Corsica are much nearer. There may be advantages in a single flight to the breeding areas, for the earliest birds may obtain the best territories (*see* Chapter 4), but there may also be disadvantages if the weather conditions are poor when the birds arrive. Clearly, some years will favour the long-haul migrants, and others the short-haul fliers.

8

MIGRATION

Once our northern Blackcaps have moulted and laid down fat, they begin their great journey to their winter quarters. Blackcaps migrate alone and at night, so the youngster, travelling for the first time, must have innate information on how to reach its wintering area.

It is generally believed that migration first evolved among birds which lived at low latitudes but spread to higher latitudes in which they could survive for only part of the year. At low latitudes, competition for resources would have been intensive and predation pressures high. Birds which moved to higher latitudes would have experienced less competition and predation, and hence would have achieved a greater breeding success. It has been argued that most migrant species have evolved to maximize reproductive output (so called r-selected species), the most numerous species laying the most eggs in a season. By contrast, most residents have evolved a strategy for high adult survival but laying fewer eggs in a season (K-selected species). Migrants return to their breeding area when food supplies are at a peak that cannot be exploited by the few residents which have survived the rigours of the winter. Owing to competition with residents, however, migrants may be restricted to narrow habitat niches, which limits their maximum population size (O'Connor 1990). In the north, we view 'our' migrants as moving south in winter to better conditions. Perhaps we should rather consider them as tropical birds moving north in spring to exploit seasonal food supplies.

As conditions at higher latitudes improved over evolutionary time, birds would migrate further north to breed, but they tended to return to their ancestral home in winter, so that some populations of migrants nowadays cover very long distances. In Chapter 1, I mentioned the subspecies of Arctic Warbler which breeds in Alaska but returns to tropical south-east Asia for the winter. New wintering areas can evolve, however, and the Blackcaps which winter in Britain provide a recent example, as described below. The wintering range of Blackcaps in the Mediterranean region may also be recent in evolutionary terms, for the ancestral home was most probably in Africa, where all members of the eastern population still winter. Indeed, the migration patterns which we observe today must have evolved since the last ice age, when northern lands became inhabitable, at most no more than 10,000 years ago and in some cases not more than 5000 years. The Sahara Desert, such a formidable obstacle to today's long-distance migrants, was highly fertile 5000 years ago (Alerstam 1990).

The benefits of migration are clearly the food supplies available for rearing young in spring and that of allowing survival in winter. There are also obvious costs in terms of the energy needed for the long flight, the risks of being blown off course in storms, or the failure to overfly ocean or desert. There are also the dangers of predators in unknown terrain. To these can be added the perils created by man: lighthouses, gas flares on North Sea oil rigs, and intensive hunting pressure. That birds still migrate shows that, overall, the benefits outweigh the costs, but, where this is no longer so, then partial migration or sedentary behaviour may evolve. This has happened in some populations of Blackcaps.

The stimulus to migrate

Many juvenile birds have a tendency to disperse prior to true migration and the Blackcap is no exception. Some 87 per cent of British ringing recoveries of juveniles in July and August were found within 25 km of the site where they were ringed, indicating local dispersal. By September, 79 per cent of recoveries within Britain were more than 25 km from their ringing site but movements appeared random, with birds being recorded from all directions of the compass except due west (Langslow 1979). Most of the recoveries after September were from abroad. These juveniles are exploring their environment and looking for likely sites to exploit in their first breeding season. It is these birds, rather than the more conservative adults, which are the pioneers in any range expansion.

True migration is directional. Migrating birds have internal annual cycles, known as 'circannual rhythms'. These can be demonstrated by keeping birds under constant environmental conditions, that is with a constant regime of light and dark, temperature and humidity, and food supply. Such individuals moult when they should, put on weight when they should, and show migratory restlessness, or Zugunruhe, at the appropriate time despite there being no seasonality in their experimental environment. This has been well demonstrated with Garden

Fig. 8.1 *The relationship between the amount of migratory restlessness shown by experimental groups of* Sylvia *warblers and the migratory distance to be covered. 1, Spectacled Warbler; 2, Marmora's Warbler; 3, Blackcap from Canary Islands; 4, Sardinian Warbler; 5, Dartford Warbler; 6, 7, 8, Blackcaps from southern France, West Germany and southern Finland, respectively; 9, Common Whitethroat; 10, Subalpine Warbler; 11, Lesser Whitethroat; 12, Garden Warbler; 13, Barred Warbler. Adapted from Berthold (1984)*

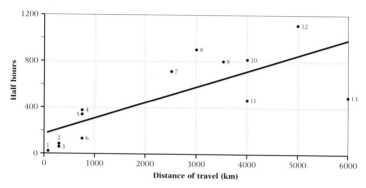

Warblers (Berthold 1988b). The seasonal events therefore appear to be programmed into the bird, although the physiological basis remains a matter of speculation. These circannual rhythms must be adjusted to the appropriate seasons by some external factor, and day length (photoperiod) acts as the synchronizer, or *Zeitgeber*. In *Sylvia* warblers, photoperiod is the only synchronizer to have been demonstrated experimentally: Garden Warblers and Sardinian Warblers were subjected to two photoperiodic cycles over a calendar-year and they showed twice the frequency of moult and migratory activity (Berthold 1988a).

Circannual rhythms may be particularly important in determining the onset of migration in spring from tropical areas, when photoperiod remains constant. Internal rhythms and photoperiod may control the onset of migration, but there are also environmental modifiers which will prevent a bird from migrating should conditions be unsuitable. These include nutrition, the deposition of fat and the amount of light at night, all of which have been determined by experiment on *Sylvia* warblers.

The amount of migratory restlessness demonstrated by *Sylvia* warblers is directly related to the distance to be covered on migration (Figure 8.1). This restlessness under experimental conditions consists of flying, hopping, fluttering and wing-whirring, this last probably a substitute for flight in caged birds. Non-migratory Spectacled Warblers show little restlessness, whereas the highly migratory Garden and Barred Warblers show the most. Within the Blackcaps, different populations showed different amounts of restlessness. Thus the non-migratory Canary Islands Blackcaps exhibited little restlessness, while those from southern Finland showed the most. The total period of migratory restlessness during experiments was sufficient to allow birds to reach their winter quarters had they been free to fly; that is, there is an endogenous programme for migration distance. Female Blackcaps showed significantly longer migratory restlessness than males, and this is consistent with differences in migration distance demonstrated in the wild (Berthold 1992).

Navigation

Birds may find their way on migration by use of a sun-compass, a star-compass, a magnetic-compass, or a combination of these. They can also follow landmarks, although evidence suggests that these are used only when birds are close to their goal.

The star-compass has been demonstrated in Blackcaps by placing them in a planetarium, in which the pattern of the stars was projected on to a dome-shaped roof. The birds orientated in their natural migration direction in relation to the stars, and, when the pattern of the stars in the planetarium was reversed, the orientation of the birds also reversed. The position of the stars, of course, shift through the night. How does a bird compensate for this? Detailed studies of the Indigo Bunting in North America have shown that the birds take their bearings in relation to the Pole Star, which lies always due north, using the patterns of constellations around the Pole Star to determine the direction north. Such a star-compass does not depend on an internal clock. There is, however, some evidence that *Sylvia* warblers use a time-compensated star-compass which is based on stars near the celestial equator (Alerstam 1990). There may be an advantage in this for long-distance migrants, because the Pole Star is not visible near the Equator. Indigo Buntings remain all year in the northern hemisphere.

The presence of a magnetic-compass has also been demonstrated in the Blackcap and a range of other species. The magnetic-compass of a bird uses the axial course of the field lines and their inclination in space (a dip-compass), so that the bird distinguishes between the direction towards the pole and the direction towards

the Equator, rather than between north and south, as our compasses do. Furthermore, the bird's compass is continually being finely adjusted to the surrounding magnetic field, making for accurate navigation. Birds have crystals of magnetite in their brains. Hand-reared Garden Warblers that have seen neither stars nor sun can find their migration direction by magnetic clues alone. Conversely, Garden Warblers that had watched a night sky during their development could orientate by the stars in the absence of any magnetic experience. So, the birds are capable of navigating using either the stars or the magnetic field.

How do these mechanisms interact? Experiments with Garden Warblers and Robins, involving both adjusting the magnetic field under a natural sky and adjusting the sky under a natural magnetic field, showed that, during migration, magnetic information dominated over information from the stars. During the early life of the bird however, the star-compass dominated and was calibrated independently of the magnetic field. It appears that there is a change in the control of the star-compass, from celestial rotation during development to the magnetic field during migration. The reason for this may be that, as the birds migrate south, their familiar stars descend and finally disappear over the horizon, to be replaced by new constellations. By contrast, the magnetic field has a regular north–south course and can be used to calibrate new configurations of stars (Wiltschko and Wiltschko 1988).

There is also evidence from some species that nocturnal migrants may also use the sun. The point at which the sun sets in the west could be used to calibrate the positions of the stars, but, as this point varies with both latitude and season, there may be an interaction between the sunset point and the magnetic field. The interactions between the cues which control the orientation of any night migrant are still very imperfectly understood.

The east–west divide

Populations of Blackcaps in Europe show a migratory divide (Figure 8.2). Western birds generally fly south-west in autumn to southern France, Iberia and the Maghreb, with a variable number flying on to West Africa. Those from central and eastern Europe (east of 10–11 °E) fly south-east to the eastern Mediterranean and

Fig. 8.2 *Migration routes of the Blackcap. The main routes are indicated by thick lines, subsidiary routes by thin lines. Adapted from Berthold (1988a)*

then head south-west to East Africa. This has been shown from ringing recoveries and from placing hand-reared Blackcaps in orientation cages in Germany (Helbig *et al.* 1989). In the cages, West German birds orientated south-west during the entire migration season. Austrian birds orientated south-east in October and south-west in November, the shift in direction of 60° taking place during a ten-day period between 25 October and 5 November.

Genetical control of migration

It is clear that much of the migratory behaviour of Blackcaps and indeed of many other birds, is under genetic control. To explain the migration of *Sylvias*, the 'vector-navigation hypothesis' has been developed (Berthold 1988a). This proposes that circannual rhythms initially cause inexperienced juveniles to deposit fat and begin migration at the correct time. They are able to find the winter quarters of their population by migrating along their specific vectors, using inherited migration programmes, which are composed of an internal time programme and a programmed direction, until their migratory activity ceases. They would then automatically have reached their wintering area. Can birds cover such long distances under genetic control when so many environmental variables may impede the speed and direction of migration? It is argued that birds on southward migration fly only for a few hours and for relatively short distances of only 50 km each night, so that forced stops should not upset the overall migration programme (Berthold 1991). Backup systems operate if things do not go according to plan. Migrants which exhaust their fuel supplies, for example, can stay in one place for relatively long periods to replenish them.

The genetical basis of a number of aspects of Blackcap migration has been studied by cross-breeding experiments. Such studies, undertaken to elucidate moult patterns, have already been described in Chapter 7. The genetic control of migratory restlessness was examined by mating Blackcaps from the Canary Islands with those from South Germany. Canary Islands birds exhibit restlessness for about 50 days, and South German birds for just over 150 days. Their hybrid offspring showed restlessness for about 125 days (Berthold 1988b).

Some populations of Blackcaps are only partially migratory; some individuals migrate, while others do not. Is the individual's strategy genetically determined, or does it depend on environmental or social conditions? To examine this, a breeding experiment was carried out with birds from the Rhône valley in southern France, where 75 per cent of the population is migratory and 25 per cent resident (Berthold 1988c). Selective breeding was carried out, mating together either migrants or residents. With selective breeding of non-migrants, the population became exclusively resident within six generations. It took just three generations of selective breeding of migrants to produce a completely migratory population. Thus, this partially migratory population would be able to adapt its migration strategy extremely rapidly in response to changing environmental conditions.

Partial migration appears to have evolved here to reduce competition during winter. It was observed that the population density in winter was higher than that in the summer and there were many competitive interactions over food. At least 25 per cent of the winter population were northern birds, which are larger and presumably stronger than the locals. Young birds, and especially females, of the local population were poorly represented in winter, and it is suggested that these, the weakest group, migrate in order to avoid competition with their stronger northern relatives.

The population of Blackcaps in the Cape Verde Islands is fully resident. Nestlings were transferred to Germany and hand-reared. In the following year, they were mated with migratory German birds. Of 35 hybrids produced, 38 per cent exhibited migratory activity equivalent to 70 per cent of the activity of their German parents. They also showed the correct direction of migration in autumn.

To show that migratory direction is also under genetic control, cross-breeding experiments have again been performed (Helbig 1991a). Blackcaps from West Germany, which migrate south-westwards, and birds from eastern Austria, which migrate south-eastwards, were taken from nests when 7–8 days old and hand-reared. When they became restless in autumn, they were each tested several times for their migration direction. They were placed in round, funnel-shaped cages lined with typewriter correction paper, and the scratches recorded on the paper the next morning indicated the desired direction of migration. They showed the expected pattern. West German birds headed south-west; Austrian birds headed south-east in October and south-west in November, which would take them to Asia Minor and then on to East Africa. The following spring, individuals from the two populations were mated and 16 pairs produced a total of 68 hybrid offspring. In the autumn the hybrids were tested, and they showed orientation intermediate in direction between those of their parents.

The change in direction made naturally in October-November by Austrian parents was also expressed in the hybrid young but was much smaller in extent. Migratory direction is clearly under genetic control.

In central Europe, there is likely to be an overlap zone between these two migratory populations and some mixed pairs could form naturally. It was predicted that their offspring would attempt to cross the Alps, the Mediterranean and the Sahara Desert, hazards avoided by the majority of parents of both populations. There is therefore likely to be strong selection against these hybrids because they would have such a low chance of survival.

When Blackcaps from this central area were hand-reared and tested for orientation direction, the results were very surprising (Helbig 1991b, 1992). These birds were collected from Linz, in west Austria, midway between the places of origin of birds used in the previous experiment. The Linz birds oriented from south-west to north-west, significantly different from the populations on each side (Figure 8.3), so that, rather than being a mixture of the strategies of the two populations, they were clearly differentiated. Indeed, it appears that this population is the one that winters in the British Isles. The habit of wintering in Britain and Ireland on a regular basis has evolved over the last 25–30 years and, as already discussed, the wintering population has increased greatly over this time. To prove that British birds were likely to be from this population, 40 Blackcaps (20 each of males and females) were captured in winter near to Weston-super-Mare in south-west England and transported to Germany. Here they produced 41 young which were hand-reared. Their direction of orientation in autumn, and that of their parents, was determined in orientation chambers and compared with West German birds hand-raised in the same

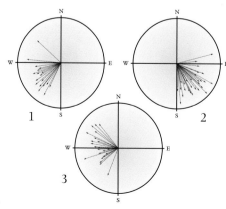

Fig. 8.3

Orientation direction of hand-raised Blackcaps from populations in 1) West Germany (Radolfzell), 2) eastern Austria (Burgenland) and 3) western Austria (Linz). Adapted from Helbig (1991b)

way. The German birds took the classic south-west route, whereas the parents caught in Weston-super-Mare and their young headed north of west (Berthold *et al.* 1992). Large numbers of Blackcaps have been ringed in central Europe but, prior to 1961, none had been recovered to the north-west. Now such occurrences make up 7–11 per cent of the recoveries in parts of Germany and Austria.

This area of central Europe can be considered as a 'hybrid zone' between two populations which differ genetically in respect of their migration directions. Once the new migration pattern to the north-west had evolved, it was likely to spread rapidly through the population, especially as hybrids adopting an intermediate southerly migration strategy would be strongly selected against, as described above.

The new wintering area is 1000–1500 km north of the traditional Blackcap wintering areas in the western Mediterranean. For birds to reach Britain, however, the angle of normal migration, which spans some 140° from south-east to south-west, need only be increased by 30°. This direction was previously strongly selected against but it is now strongly selected for (Berthold and Terrill 1988), presumably because of improved conditions for survival in Britain in winter. Such conditions may include an amelioration in climate and better feeding opportunities, especially as many more people now feed birds in Britain in winter and Blackcaps are regular bird table visitors. There will also be less competition for food between individual Blackcaps than in the highly populated Mediterranean region. The migration distance to Britain is also about a third less, with an obvious decrease in the associated energetic costs. It is also likely that the shorter day lengths experienced by British wintering birds could result in an earlier migration and breeding season. In the winter, birds enter a refractory period and fail to come into reproductive condition, even when exposed to photoperiod regimes that stimulated reproduction earlier in the year. Short day lengths, however, end this refractory period. Arrival on the breeding grounds from Britain could be ten days earlier than it is for birds returning from the Mediterranean, allowing males to select the best territories. Because British winterers have adapted to a cold winter, they may be better able to withstand inclement weather early in the breeding season. As they arrive early, males and females from Britain are likely to inter-breed, and this, together with better breeding success associated with early breeding on higher-quality territories, is likely to be the reason for the rapid spread of this new migratory direction in the central European population.

These detailed studies of hand-raised birds in Germany have shown that most of the physiology and behaviour of Blackcaps is genetically determined, although this does not preclude individuals from responding to particular environmental conditions. This genetic control should not be surprising, because, in such short-lived birds, the opportunity for learning and experience must be very limited. The studies have also shown, however, that, through natural selection, populations can respond quickly to changing environmental conditions. They demonstrate evolution in action. Thus, if the dire predictions concerning the 'greenhouse effect' prove to be true, the Blackcap is one species at least which may respond rapidly to the changed conditions.

The journey south

The Blackcap can be described as a leapfrog migrant, the northern populations flying furthest south to the southern edge of the wintering range. They have longer wings and put on more weight than their more southerly counterparts, and they also migrate at higher altitudes (Bruderer and Jenni 1990). They also begin migration earlier, for more are caught at a Swiss ringing station at the beginning of the migration season when many local birds are still moulting (Turrian and Jenni 1989).

Evidence from central Europe suggests that Blackcaps move south in rather short nocturnal flight stages of 50 km, each of which may take little more than an hour's flying, until they reach an ecological barrier such as sea or desert. Unless conditions preclude migration, they rarely spend more than a day in any one locality. Blackcaps are capable of much longer flights, however, and it is thought that British birds make a non-stop flight of some 800 km to south-west France and north-east Spain – no Blackcaps have been recovered in north and central France, in contrast to Sedge Warblers, whose autumn recoveries are concentrated there (Langslow 1979). The average weight (19.3 g) of Blackcaps in late summer at a ringing site in southern England suggests that they carry sufficient fats to make this journey without difficulty (Phillips 1994). The longest journey recorded for a British Blackcap in a single day was 281 km, while the greatest known distance covered by an individual is 5000 km.

Young birds begin to disperse in early July, and adults from mid-July onwards. Most leave Britain from late August through September, and appear to cross the English Channel at the narrow south-east end before heading south-west. By October, they are well distributed in south-west France and north-east Spain, with records as far south as Morocco. Most British Blackcaps appear to winter in southern Spain and North Africa, although some winter south of the Sahara, with recoveries in Senegal and Guinea, Guinea-Bissau and Mauritania.

At British bird observatories there are considerable numbers of Blackcaps in October, with some through November, and these are undoubtedly Continental in origin. Birds prefer to migrate when they have favourable tailwinds and they tend to avoid areas of rainfall. Conditions may change, however, during migration. The large falls of migrants at bird observatories occur when there are anticyclones over Scandinavia coinciding with frontal systems carrying cloud across the North Sea. Birds leaving Scandinavia on a course west of south are carried west by easterly winds and they will alight as soon as they can, on the British coast. Once weather conditions improve, they will reorientate and continue migration. Some of these incomers, however, will be Blackcaps which winter in Britain and Ireland.

The peak passage through northern Italy is in the first half of October, in southern Spain it is in the last ten days of the month, while in Gibraltar the peak passage is from mid-October to mid-November (Schubert et al. 1986; Rodriguez 1985; Finlayson 1992). Most recoveries from North Africa are not until January, confirming a leisurely migration through Iberia (Fouarge 1981b).

Those populations which migrate south-east pass through Turkey mainly in September. There are peaks at the end of September and in early October in Cyprus, Syria and Israel, and Blackcaps are present in East Africa from late October.

Crossing the desert

The two major ecological barriers facing migrant birds are seas and deserts. Seas clearly must be crossed in one go or birds will perish. Some, of course, hitch lifts on boats, as anyone making a ferry crossing of the North Sea in the migration period will be aware. Some of these birds will be exhausted, and the boat is a lifeline. Some just find it convenient, while others may be attracted in by the lights at night and stay. On sight of land, they mostly abandon ship.

Those Blackcaps which cross the Sahara Desert face, as do their fellow migrants, a distance of some 1500 km, at a time when mean daily maximum temperatures are in the region of 25–30 °C, while temperatures on the desert surface may approach

Ships provide welcome resting places for tired migrants.

70 °C. The relative humidity of the air may fall to 10 per cent. It has always been assumed that migrants attempt to cross the desert in a single flight and put on sufficient fat for a journey from southern Europe across both the Mediterranean Sea and the Sahara, a single crossing of 2200–2500 km, taking 40–60 hours. Some birds may break the journey in the rich feeding grounds of North Africa. Those birds which are recorded at oases were considered to be individuals that, for some reason, miscalculated.

Recent observations in the desert have indicated, however, that this may not be the strategy adopted by small passerines, or at least not the only strategy. Many birds have been found resting during the day in the desert with adequate fat for them to continue their journey; they appear to be seeking shade and are quite content with small areas. In contrast, birds found in the larger oases are generally lighter, feed actively, and stay for several days, whereas the fat birds leave at dusk. When placed in cages in the shade, with food and water provided *ad libitum*, light individuals of several species fed intensively during the day and rested at night, whereas fat individuals completely ignored food and water but became active at night (Barlein 1992). Could this, then, be the normal strategy for crossing the desert, an intermittent migration with rests during the day and flight at night? This would be a continuation of the short-hop strategy adopted while moving south

Savanna forest at the end of the dry season in the Gambia, an area supporting numbers of Blackcaps in winter.

Stones provide shelter from the desert sun.

across Europe, and it would fit in with the periods of restlessness shown by caged warblers held in Germany throughout the migration season. As Wood (1989) has argued, however, if all individuals did this, then, large numbers of migrants would be found at times in the desert but they are not.

Biebach (1990, 1992) has suggested that wind and temperature will have a major influence on the way small passerines cross the desert. Normally birds encounter a tailwind on autumn migration across the Sahara. During the daytime if there is a tailwind to 3000m there will be a headwind above 3000 m. Air temperature decreases with altitude, to reach 10 °C at 3000 m during the day and at 1000 m at night, and birds must fly at temperatures of 10° or less to maintain their water budget. Under these conditions, birds can fly at the optimum temper-ature in a tailwind to cross the desert in a single journey. If wind conditions change, however, such that headwinds are encoun-tered at lower altitudes then the bird has a problem. It can fly at 3000 m to conserve water but wastes energy battling against the wind, or it can fly at a lower altitude in a tailwind but lose water. In these conditions it is preferable to rest in the shade during the day and to migrate at night, when flight is possible at a lower altitude where tailwinds are more likely. The strategy adopted by an individual crossing the Sahara will depend on the weather conditions applying at the time.

As has already been described, a large proportion of western Blackcaps avoids this crossing altogether by wintering in the Mediterranean region. The eastern population, however, has to cross both the Sinai and the Sahara Deserts.

Winter movements

Once they have reached their wintering area, many species become quite sedentary. Blackcaps, however, behave differently and this must be related to the supplies of fruit, which vary seasonally and geographically from year to year. In southern France, Robins, Dunnocks and Firecrests were regularly recaptured at a ringing site through the winter, illustrating long periods of sedentary behaviour, but few Blackcaps were recaptured (Debussche and Isenmann 1984). On Gibraltar, passage is often recorded in December and January (Finlayson 1992) as birds seek good feeding areas. Fluctuations over the winter are also recorded in both West and East Africa. In the latter region, Blackcaps often forage in small parties, frequently with other forest species (Pearson 1978). If food supplies in any one area are good, however, Blackcaps will settle down and some will actively defend patches of good resources, as described in Chapter 5.

Spring migration

In late winter in East Africa, some Blackcaps become territorial and establish song posts. The birds leave rather abruptly in late March, and they are rarely seen after the first week in April (Pearson 1978). Northward migration proceeds more rapidly than the autumn movements, birds taking only six weeks to reach their breeding areas from southern Africa (Pearson and Lack 1992): the earliest arrivals are likely to get the good territories and have, therefore, both the best resources and the most time in which to rear young.

In Gibraltar, there are heavy northward movements of Blackcaps during February and early March, with males leaving earlier than females. Passage continues into early May, these later birds probably being trans-Saharan migrants (Finlayson 1992). In southern Spain, spring migration lasts over 80 days from early March to the end of May, with peak passage from mid-March to the end of the first week in April (Rodriguez 1985).

The very first arrivals of Blackcaps in southern Britain are in March, but the peak passage is in late April and early May. On Fair Isle the peak is in late May and early June, and similar late activity is seen at east-coast observatories; these must be birds of Scandinavian origin which have overshot their breeding area (Riddiford and Findleyson 1981). Following the first arrivals in early April, British woodlands ring with the songs of Blackcaps by the end of the month, and the cycle of life begins anew.

Bibliography

Alerstam, T., *Bird Migration*, Cambridge University Press, Cambridge, 1990

Ash, J.S., *Ibis* 111 (1969) 1–10

Ash, J.S., Jones, P.H., and Melville, R., *British Birds* 54 (1961) 93–100

Baillie, S.R., and Peach, W.J., *Ibis* 134, supplement 1 (1992) 120–32

Baldeschi, P., *Gli Uccelli* 6 (1981) 171–4

Barlein, F., *Journal für Ornithologie* 119 (1978) 14–51

Barlein, F., *Ornis Scandinavica* 14 (1983) 239–45

Barlein, F., *Ibis* 134, supplement 1 (1992) 41–6

Barlein, F., Berthold, P., Querner, U., and Schlenker, R., *Journal für Ornithologie* 121 (1980) 325–69

Benson, G.B.G., and Williamson, K., *Bird Study* 19 (1972) 34–50

Berthold, P., *Journal für Ornithologie* 117 (1976a), 145–209

Berthold, P., *Ardea* 64 (1976b) 140–54

Berthold, P., *Bird Study* 31 (1984) 19–27

Berthold, P., *Tauraco* 1 (1988a) 3–28

Berthold, P., *Proceedings of the 19th International Ornithological Congress, Ottawa*, 1988b, pp. 215-49

Berthold, P., *Journal of Evolutionary Biology* 1 (1988c) 195–209

Berthold, P., in *Orientation in Birds* (ed. P. Berthold), Birkhauser, Basel, 1991, pp. 86–105

Berthold, P., *Ibis* 134, supplement 1 (1992) 35–40

Berthold, P., Helbig, A.J., Mohr, G., and Querner, U., *Nature* 360 (1992) 668–70

Berthold, P., and Querner, U., *Experentia* 38 (1982) 801–2

Berthold, P., and Schlenker, R., 'Mönchgrasmücke', in *Handbuch der Vögel Mitteleuropas*, vol. 12/2 (ed. U.N. Glutz von Blotzheim and K.M. Bauer), Aula-Verlag, Wiesbaden, 1991, pp. 949-1020

Berthold, P., and Terrill, S.B., *Ringing and Migration* 9 (1988) 153–9

Bibby, C.J., *Ibis* 134, supplement 1 (1992) 29–34

Bibby, C.J., Phillips, B.N., and Seddon, A.J.E., *Journal of Applied Ecology* 22 (1985) 619–33

Biebach, H., in *Bird Migration* (ed. E. Gwinner), Springer-Verlag, Berlin, 1990, pp. 352–67

Biebach, H., *Ibis* 134, supplement 1 (1992) 47–54

Birkhead, T.R., *The Magpies*, Poyser, London, 1991

Boddy, M., *Bird Study* 38 (1991) 188–99

Bongiorno, S.F., *Ibis* 124 (1982) 1–20

Bruderer, B., and Jenni, L., in *Bird Migration* (ed. E. Gwinner), Springer-Verlag, Berlin, 1990, pp. 60-77

Bull, A.L., Mead, C.J., and Williamson, K., *Bird Study* 23 (1976) 163–82

Calvario, E., Fraticelli, F., Gustin, M., Sarrocco, S., and Sorace, A., *Avocetta* 13 (1989) 53–5

Carah, P., *British Birds* 54 (1961) 124

Cody, M.L., *Ecological Monographs* 48 (1978) 351–96

Cody, M.L., and Walter, H., *Oikos* 27 (1976) 210–38

Cramp, S. (ed.) *The Birds of the Western Palearctic Vol. VI*, Oxford University Press, Oxford, 1992

Crick, H.Q.P., Gibbons, D.W., and Magrath, R.D., *Journal of Animal Ecology* 62 (1993a) 263–73

Crick, H.Q.P., Dudley, C. ,and Glue, D., *BTO News* 185 (1993b) 15–18

Cuadrado, M., *Ringing and Migration* 13 (1992) 36–42

Cuadrado, M., Rodriguez, M., and Arjona, S., *Ringing and Migration* 10 (1989) 89–97

Davis, P., *Bird Study* 14 (1967), 65–95

Debussche, M., and Isenmann, P., *L'Oiseau* 54 (1984) 101–7

Deckert, G., *Journal für Ornithologie* 96 (1955) 186–206

de Naurois, R., and Bergier, P., *Cyanopica* 3 (1986) 517–31

Diesselhorst, G., *Bonner Zoologische Beiträge* 19 (1968) 307–31

Edington, J.M., and Edington, M.A., *Journal of Animal Ecology* 41 (1972) 331–57

Ellegren, H., and Fransson, T., *Ringing and Migration* 13 (1992) 1–12

Elton, C., *Animal Ecology*, Sidgwick and Jackson, London, 1927

Farina, A., *Avocetta*, 6 (1982) 75–81

Fenech, N., *Fatal Flight: the Maltese Obsession with Killing Birds*, Quiller Press, London, 1992

Ferry, C., and Frochot, B., *La Terre et la Vie* 2 (1970) 153–250

Ferry, C., Frochot, B., and Leruth, Y., *Studies in Avian Biology* 6 (1981) 119–20

Finlayson, J.C., *Ibis* 123 (1981) 88–95

Finlayson, J.C., *Birds of the Strait of Gibraltar*, Poyser, Calton, 1992

Ford, H.A., *Bird Study* 34 (1987) 205–18

Fouarge, J., *Aves* 17 (1981a) 17–27

Fouarge, J., *Le Gerfaut* 71 (1981b) 677–716

Fraticelli, F., and Sarrocco, S., *Avocetta* 8 (1984) 91–8

Fuller, R.J., *Bird Habitats in Great Britain*, Poyser, Calton, 1982

Fuller, R.J., in *Ecology and Management of Coppice Woodlands* (ed. G.P. Buckley), Chapman and Hall, London, 1992, pp. 169–92

Fuller, R.J., and Henderson, A.C.B., *Bird Study* 39 (1992) 73–88

Fuller, R.J., and Moreton, B.D., *Journal of Applied Ecology* 24 (1987) 13–27

Fuller, R.J., Stuttard, P., and Ray, C.M., *Annales Zoologici Fennici* 26 (1989) 265–75

Fuller, R.J. and Whittington, P.A., *Acta Oecologia/Oecologia Generalis* 8 (1987) 259–68

Garcia, E.F.J., 'An experimental and observational study of interspecific territoriality between the Blackcap *Sylvia atricapilla* (Linnaeus) and the Garden Warbler *Sylvia borin* (Boddaert)' (University of Oxford D. Phil. thesis, 1981)

Garcia, E.F.J., *Journal of Animal Ecology* 52 (1983) 795–805

Garcia, E., *The Blackcap and the Garden Warbler*, Shire Publications, Aylesbury, 1989

Gibbons, D.W., Reid, J.B., and Chapman, R.A., *The New Atlas of Breeding Birds in Britain and Ireland: 1988–1991*, Poyser, London, 1993

Gilbert, D.C., *British Birds* 79 (1986) 405–6

Gladwin, T.W., *Bird Study* 16 (1969) 131–2

Glue, D., *The Garden Bird Book*, Macmillan, London, 1982

Glue, D., *British Birds* 78 (1985) 354

Gnielka, R., *Beiträge zur Vogelkunde* 33 (1987) 103–13

Gosler, A., *The Great Tit*, Hamlyn, London, 1993

Greenoak, F., *All the Birds of the Air*, Penguin Books, London, 1979

Groebbels, F., *Der Vogel: Bau, Funktion, Lebenserscheinung, Einpassung*, Vol. 1, Borntraeger, Berlin, 1932

Haartman, L.V. *Commentationes Biologicae* 32 (1969) 3–187

Hardy, E., *Bird Study* 25 (1978) 60–1

Harper, D., *British Birds* 79 (1986) 136–7

Harrison, C., *An Atlas of the Birds of the Western Palearctic*, Collins, London, 1982

Heim de Balsac, H., and Mayaud, N.,

Alauda 2 (1930) 474–93

Helbig, A.J., *Behavioural Ecology and Sociobiology* 28 (1991a) 9–12

Helbig, A.J., *Journal of Evolutionary Biology* 4 (1991b) 653–70

Helbig, A.J., *Oecologia* 90 (1992) 483–8

Helbig, A.J., Berthold, P., and Wiltschko, W., *Ethology* 82 (1989) 307–15

Herremans, M., *Ringing and Migration* 10 (1989) 31–4

Herremans, M., *Ringing and Migration* 12 (1991) 75–9

Herrera, C.M., *Ecological Monographs* 54 (1984) 1–23

Hickling, R., *Enjoying Ornithology*, Poyser, Calton, 1983

Hodson, N.L., and Snow, D.W., *Bird Study* 12 (1965) 90–9

Hölzinger, J., *Journal für Ornithologie* 131 (1990) 167–71

Howard, H.E., *The British Warblers*, London, 1907-14

Howard, E., *Territory in Bird Life*, Murray, London, 1920

Ioale, P. and Benvenuti, S., *Avocetta* 6 (1982) 63–74

Jordano, P., *Oikos* 38 (1982) 183–93

Jordano, P., *Ardea* 76 (1988) 193–209

Jordano, P., and Herrera, C., *Ibis* 123 (1981) 502–7

Kaiser, A., *Bird Study* 39 (1992) 96–110

Keen, S.G., *British Birds* 82 (1989) 117–8

Labitte, A., *L'Oiseau* 25 (1955) 308–11

Lack, P., *The Atlas of Wintering Birds in Britain and Ireland*, Poyser, Calton, 1986

Lack, P.C., *Annales Zoologici Fennici* 26 (1989) 219–25

Lack, P., *Birds on Lowland Farms*, HMSO, London, 1992

La Mantia, T., *Avocetta* 6 (1982) 41–6

Lambertini, M., *Avocetta* 5 (1981) 65–86

Langslow, D.R., *Ringing and Migration* 1 (1976) 78–91

Langslow, D.R., *British Birds* 71 (1978) 345–354

Langslow, D.R., *Bird Study* 26 (1979) 239–52

Laursen, K., *Ornis Scandinavica* 9 (1978) 178–92

Leach, I.H., *Bird Study* 28 (1981) 5–14

Linsell, S.E., *British Birds* 42 (1949) 294

Lo Valvo, F., Lo Verde, G., and Lo Valvo, M., *Ringing and Migration* 9 (1988) 51–4

MacArthur, R.H., *Ecology* 39 (1958) 599–619

Macdonald, D., *British Birds* 71 (1978) 132–3

Macdonald, S.M. and Mason, C.F., *British Birds* 66 (1973) 361–3

Magnin, G., in *Conserving Migratory Birds* (ed. T. Salathé), ICBP, Cambridge, 1991, pp. 59-71

Marchant, J.H., Hudson, R., Carter, S.P., and Whittington, P., *Population Trends in British Breeding Birds*, BTO, Tring, 1990

Mason, C.F., *Bird Study* 23 (1976) 213–32

Mason, C.F., and Hussey, A., *Ringing and Migration* 5 (1984) 113–20

Mason, C.F., and Long, S.P., in *Countryside Monitoring and Management* (ed. R. Matthews), Countryside Commission, Manchester, 1987, pp. 37–42

Massa, B., *Revista Italiana di Ornitologia* 51 (1981) 167–78

McCullough, M.N., Tucker, G.M., and Baillie, S.R., *Ibis* 134, supplement 1 (1992) 55–65

Moreau, R.E., *Bird Study* 17 (1970) 95–103

Morel, G.J., and Morel, M-Y., *Ibis* 134, supplement 1 (1992) 83–8

Morgan, R., *Bird Study* 22 (1975) 71–83

Moritz, D., *Vogelwelt* 103 (1982) 129–43

Morris, F.O., *A History of British Birds*, Groombridge and Sons, London, 1860

Newton, I., *The Sparrowhawk*, Poyser,

Calton, 1986

Nilsson, S.G., *Oikos* 28 (1977) 170–6

Norman, S.C., *Ringing and Migration* 11 (1990) 12–22

O'Connor, R.J., in *Bird Migration* (ed. E. Gwinner), Springer-Verlag, Berlin, 1990, pp. 175–82

Österlöf, S., and Stolt, B-O., *Ornis Scandinavica* 13 (1982) 135–140

Parmenter, T., and Byers, C., *A Guide to the Warblers of the Western Palearctic*, Bruce Coleman, Uxbridge, 1991

Parsons, A.J., *Bird Study* 23 (1976) 287–93

Pearson, D.J., *Bird Study* 20 (1973) 24–36

Pearson, D.J., *Scopus* 2 (1978) 63–71

Pearson, D.J., and Lack, P.C., *Ibis* 134, supplement 1 (1992) 89–98

Persson, B., *Ambio* 1 (1972) 34–5

Pfister, H.P., Naef, B., and Blum, H., *Ornithologische Beobachter* 83 (1986) 7–34

Phillips, N.J., *Ringing and Migration*, 15 (1994) 17–26

Piacentini, J., and Thibault, J.C., *Alauda* 59 (1991) 155–62

Rackham, O., *Trees and Woodland in the British Landscape*, Dent, London, 1976

Raines, R.J., *British Birds* 38 (1945) 202–4

Riddiford, N., and Findley, P., *Seasonal Movements of Summer Migrants*, BTO, Tring, 1981

Rodriguez, M., *Ringing and Migration* 6 (1985) 33–8

Rodriguez de los Santos, M., Cuadrado, M., and Arjona, S., *Bird Study*, 33 (1986) 81–6

Schubert, M., Fedrigo, A., and Massa, R., *Ringing and Migration* 7 (1986) 15-22

Sharrock, J.T.R., *The Atlas of Breeding Birds in Britain and Ireland*, BTO, Tring, 1976

Shrubb, M., *Bird Study* 17 (1970) 123–44

Siefke, A., *Dorn- und Zaungrasmücke*, Neue Brehm-Bücherei, Wittenberg Lutherstadt, 1962

Simms, E., *Woodland Birds*, Collins, London, 1971

Simms, E., *British Warblers*, Collins, London, 1985

Snow, B. and Snow, D., *Birds and Berries*, Poyser, Calton, 1988

Thom, V., *Birds in Scotland*, Poyser, Calton, 1986

Thompson, P., *BTO News* 166 (1990) 7

Tomialojc, L., Wesolowski, T., and Walankiewicz, W., *Acta Ornithologica* 20 (1984) 241–310

Turrian, F., and Jenni, L., *Alauda* 57 (1989) 133–54

Turrian, F., and Jenni, L., *Alauda* 59 (1991) 73–88

Tutman, I., *Vogelwelt* 90 (1969) 169–79

Ulfstrand, S., and Högstedt, G., *Anser* 15 (1976) 1–32

Williamson, K., *Bird Study* 18 (1971a) 225–6

Williamson, K., *Bird Study* 18 (1971b) 80–96

Williamson, K., *Bird Study* 22 (1975) 59–70

Williamson, R., and Williamson, K., *British Birds* 66 (1973) 12–23

Wiltschko, W. and Wiltschko, R., *Trends in Ecology and Evolution* 3 (1988) 13–15

Wood, B., *Ibis* 124 (1982) 66–72

Wood, B., *Ringing and Migration* 10 (1989) 48–52

Wyllie, I., *Bird Study* 23 (1976) 39–50

Wyllie, I., *The Cuckoo*, Batsford, London,

Scientific Names

BIRDS

Wigeon *Anas penelope*
Sparrowhawk *Accipiter nisus*
Eleonora's Falcon *Falco eleonorae*
Woodpigeon *Columba palumbus*
Cuckoo *Cuculus canorus*
Wryneck *Jynx torquilla*
Great Spotted Woodpecker *Picoides
(Dendrocopos) major*
Lesser Spotted Woodpecker
P. (D.) minor
Sand Martin *Riparia riparia*
Swallow *Hirundo rustica*
Yellow Wagtail *Motacilla flava*
Wren *Troglodytes troglodytes*
Dunnock *Prunella modularis*
Robin *Erithacus rubecula*
Nightingale *Luscinia megarhynchos*
Redstart *Phoenicurus phoenicurus*
Wheatear *Oenanthe oenanthe*
Blackbird *Turdus merula*
Song Thrush *T. philomelos*
Mistle Thrush *T. viscivorus*
gnatwrens *Microbates* spp.
gnatcatchers *Polioptila* spp.
Grasshopper Warbler *Locustella
naevia*
Sedge Warbler *Acrocephalus
schoenobaenus*
Icterine Warbler *Hippolais icterina*
Barred Warbler *Sylvia nisoria*
Orphean Warbler *S. hortensis*
Arabian Warbler *S. leucomelaena*
Garden Warbler *S. borin*
Blackcap *S. atricapilla*
Common Whitethroat *S. communis*
Lesser Whitethroat *S. curruca*
Desert Warbler *S. nana*

Rüppell's Warbler *S. rüppelli*
Sardinian Warbler *S. melanocephala*
Cyprus Warbler *S. melanothorax*
Menetrie's Warbler *S. mystacea*
Subalpine Warbler *S. cantillans*
Spectacled Warbler *S. conspicillata*
Tristram's Warbler *S. deserticola*
Dartford Warbler *S. undata*
Marmora's Warbler *S. sarda*
Willow Warbler *Phylloscopus
trochilus*
Chiffchaff *P. collybita*
Bonelli's Warbler *P. bonelli*
Chinese Leaf Warbler *P. sichuanensis*
Hainan Leaf Warbler *P. hainanus*
Arctic Warbler *P. borealis*
Goldcrest *Regulus regulus*
Firecrest *R. ignicapillus*
grass warblers *Cisticola* and
Prinia spp.
Fernbird *Bowdleria punctata*
songlarks *Cinclorhamphus* spp.
Spinifex Bird *Eremiornis carteri*
Spotted Flycatcher *Muscicapa striata*
babblers *Timaliidae*
Long-tailed Tit *Aegithalos caudatus*
Great Tit *Parus major*
Nuthatch *Sitta europaea*
Jay *Garrulus glandarius*
Magpie *Pica pica*
Carrion Crow *Corvus corone*
Starling *Sturnus vulgaris*
Chaffinch *Fringilla coelebs*
Bullfinch *Pyrrhula pyrrhula*
Hawfinch *Coccothraustes
coccothraustes*
wood-warblers *Parulidae (Dendroica)*
Indigo Bunting *Passerina cyanea*

MAMMALS
squirrels *Sciurus*
Stoat *Mustela erminea*
Weasel *M. nivalis*

PLANTS
Sitka Spruce *Picea sitchensis*
Japanese Larch *Larix leptolepis*
Corsican Pine *Pinus nigra*
Maritime Pine *P. pinaster*
Juniper *Juniperus communis*
Yew *Taxus baccata*
Small-leaved Lime *Tilia cordata*
Maple *Acer campestre*
Holly *Ilex aquifolium*
Spindle *Euonymus europaeus*
Dogwood *Rhamnus catharticus*
Alder Buckthorn *Frangula alnus*
Gorse *Ulex europaeus*
Dwarf Furze *U. minor*
bramble/blackberry *Rubus aggr.*
Southern Blackberry *R. ulmifolius*
Bay Laurel *Laurus nobilis*
Bird Cherry *Prunus padus*
Blackthorn *P. spinosa*
Portuguese Laurel *P. lusitanica*
Hawthorn *Crataegus monogyna*
Sea Buckthorn *Hippophae rhamnoides*
Mistletoe *Viscum album*

Ivy *Hedera helix*
Lentisc *Pistacea lenticus*
White Bryony *Bryonia dioica*
Nettle *Urtica dioica*
Fig *Ficus carica*
birch *Betula spp.*
Alder *Alnus glutinosa*
Hornbeam *Carpinus betulus*
Hazel *Corylus avellana*
Beech *Fagus sylvatica*
Evergreen Oak *Quercus ilex*
Pedunculate Oak *Q. robur*
Sessile Oak *Q. petraea*
Sweet Chestnut *Castanea sativa*
Goat Willow *Salix caprea*
Strawberry Tree *Arbutus unedo*
Ash *Fraxinus excelsior*
Olive *Olea europaea*
Privet *Ligustrum vulgare*
Woody Nightshade *Solanum
dulcamara*
Madder *Rubia peregrina*
Elder *Sambucus nigra*
Honeysuckle *Lonicera periclymenum*
Perfoliate Honeysuckle
L. caprifolium
aloe *Aloe spp.*
Winter Jasmine *Jasminum nudiflorum*
poplar *Populus spp.*
rose *Rosa spp.*

Index

Accidents 49–50
Aggression 39, 43–4, 67, 76, 82
Alarm call 91
Arrival: in spring 54–7

Bathing 92
Biometrics 15
Blackbird 24, 80, 84, 89
Breeding 54 *et seq.*; seasons 60–63; success 69
Bullfinch 77
Bunting, Indigo 105

Call-notes 90–91
Cat, as predator 49
Chaffinch 24, 27
Character convergence 89
Circannual rhythm 103
Clutch: second 63; size 61, 63–5
Cock nest 57
Common Bird Census 46
Compass: in navigation 105
Coppice management: and bird densities 29–34
Courtship 57–8; feeding 60
Crow, Carrion 69
Cuckoo 69

Density: dependent factors 52; independent factors 52; population 24–9
Desert: as hazard 111–16
Diet 72 *et seq.*
Dispersal of juveniles 103
Distraction display 67
Distress call 91

Distribution: breeding 15–17; expansion 18; winter 18–19
Dunnock 82, 117

East-west divide of migration 106
Egg 63
Energy requirement 78

Falcon, Eleonora's 50
Fat 97–8, 100, 112
Feathers 92
Fernbird 9
Fidelity to birthplace 39
Firecrest 117
Flocking 36, 117
Foraging: egology 73–5; technique 72, 77
Frugivory 76–81, 82
Fruit dispersal 78–86

Gardens 36; feeding 81–4
Genetics: fingerprinting 41; of migration 108–12; of moult 95–6; of weight 97
Goldcrest 17
Gnatcatcher 9
Gnatwren 9
Great Tit 71
Gull as predator 50

Habitat: farmland 24; management 29–36; on migration 36; in spring 20–24; winter 36–7; woodland 20–24
Hawfinch 77

Hunting of migrants 44, 51–3, 57

Hybrid zone 111

Incubation of eggs 65
Infidelity 41
Invertebrates as food 72–4

Jay 51, 69

Key-factor analysis 53
Kinglet 9

Language 85
Laying dates 61

Magnetic compass navigation 105
Magpie 51, 69
Martin, Sand 54
Migration 99–100, 102 et seq.; direction of 109; distance of 112; evolution of 102; genetic control of 108–12; partial 109; of Sylvia warblers 13; timing of 112–13, 117
Migratory restlessness 103
Mimicry 89
Mortality 49–53
Moult 92–6; adult 94; control of 96; genetics of 96; juvenile 95; strategies 93
Muscicapidae 9

Navigation 105–6
Nectar as food 72, 80
Nest 58–60; failure 69; height 60; protection 67; sites 21, 58–60
Nestling 65–6
Niche 20, 75

Niche separation 20
Nightingale 25, 33, 89

Pesticide 50
Philopatry 39
Photoperiod 96, 104
Planetarium experiments 105
Plumage 14
Pollen as food 72
Population 34 et seq.; density 24–9; in farmland 28–9; increase 46–7; in relation to management 32–3; size 45–6; trends 45–8; in woodland 27–8
Predation 49–51, 66, 69
Productivity 69–71

Races 15–17
Rat, as predator 69
Redstart 48
Reproductive strategy 60
Ringing 49
Robin 24, 80, 89, 106, 117

Sahel region 48
Site fidelity 36
Snails as food 73
Song 85–90; diurnal variation in 88; duels 39, 87; frequency of 87; function of 85; leiern 86
Songlark 9
Sparrowhawk 50
Spinifex Bird 9
Squirrel, as predator 51, 69
Star compass 105
Starling 50, 84
Stoat, as predator 51, 69
Subsong 88
Swallow 54
Sylvia 11–13

Sylviidae 9
Sylviinae 9

Taxonomy 9–13
Territory 34–45;
    establishment 39; function
    of 38; interspecific 42–5;
    size 39–41; in winter 41–2
Thrush, Song 89
Tit, Long-tailed 59
Traffic casualties 50

Vector-navigation hypothesis
    108

Wagtail, Yellow 54
Warblers 9–10; Arabian 11;
    Arctic 9, 102; Barred 12,
    74–6, 104; Bonelli's 27;
    Chiffchaff 17, 33, 36, 44,
    54, 87; Chinese Leaf 9;
    Common Whitethroat 12,
    17, 22, 33, 44, 45, 47–8,
    50, 54–6, 59, 61, 64,
    70–71, 76, 77–8, 88, 89,
    94–5, 104; Cyprus 12;
    Dartford 12, 21, 27, 89,
    104; Desert 11; distribution
    11–13; Garden 12, 15, 17,
    21, 33, 37, 40, 43–4,
    47–8, 54–6, 59, 61, 64,
    66, 70, 73–6, 77–8, 88,
    89, 90, 94–5, 99, 103–4,

106; Grasshopper 17;
    Hainan Leaf 9; Icterine 89;
    Lesser Whitethroat 12, 21,
    45, 47–8, 54–6, 59, 61,
    64, 69, 70–71, 73–6,
    77–8, 88, 90, 95, 104;
    Marmora's 12, 21, 45, 95,
    104; Ménétrie's 11; New
    World 11, 73; Orphean 12;
    Rüppell's 12; Sardinian 12,
    21, 27, 45, 73–5, 80, 89,
    104; Sedge 17, 48, 112;
    Spectacled 12, 21, 104;
    Subalpine 12, 21, 45,
    73–5, 89, 104; Tristram's
    11; Willow 17, 24, 27, 88,
    89
Weasel as predator 51, 69, 71
Weight 97–101, 112; diurnal
    variation 98; genetic
    control 98; seasonal
    variation 98; in winter 98
Wheatear 54
Wigeon 91
Wintering in Britain 19, 100,
    110–11
Woodpecker, Lesser Spotted 89
Woodpigeon 87, 92
Wren 24, 87
Wryneck 89

Zeitgeber 104
Zugunruhe 103

NATURAL HISTORY BOOKS

A complete range of Hamlyn Natural History titles is available from all good bookshops or by mail order direct from the publisher. Payment can be made by credit card or cheque/postal order in the following ways:

BY PHONE
Phone through your order on our special *Credit Card Hotline* on **01933 414 000**. Speak to our customer service team during office hours (9 a.m. to 5 p.m.) or leave a message on the answer machine, quoting your full credit card number plus expiry date and your full name and address. Please also quote the reference number J411N12C.

BY POST
Simply fill out the order form below (photocopies are acceptable) and send it with your payment to:
Cash Sales Department,
Reed Book Services Ltd.,
P.O. Box 5,
Rushden,
Northants, NN10 6YX

J411N12C

I wish to order the following titles:

	ISBN	Price	Quantity	Total
Hamlyn Guide to the Birds of Britain and Europe	0 600 57492 X	£8.99	....	£ ....
Photographic Guide to Birds of Britain and Europe	0 600 57861 5	£9.99	....	£ ....
Where to Watch Birds in Britain and Europe	0 600 58007 5	£12.99	....	£ ....
Hamlyn Species Guide: The Kestrel	0 540 01278 5	£12.99	....	£ ....
Hamlyn Species Guide: The Barn Owl	0 600 57949 2	£12.99	....	£ ....

Add £2.00 for postage and packing if your order is worth £10.00 or less   £ ....

Grand Total £ ....

Name _____ (block capitals)

Address _____

_____ Postcode _____

I enclose a cheque/postal order for £ _____ made payable to Reed Book Services Ltd
or
Please debit my ☐ Access   ☐ Visa   ☐ American Express   ☐ Diners

account number ☐☐☐☐ ☐☐☐☐ ☐☐☐☐ ☐☐☐☐

by £ _____ Expiry date _____ Signature _____

SPECIAL OFFER: FREE POSTAGE AND PACKAGING FOR ALL ORDERS OVER £10.00, add £2.00 for p+p if your order is £10.00 or less.

Whilst every effort is made to keep our prices low, the publisher reserves the right to increase the prices at short notice.
Your order will be dispatched within 5 days, but please allow up to 28 days for delivery, subject to availability.
Registered office: Michelin House, 81 Fulham Road, London SW3 6RB.
Registered in England no 1974080.

If you do not wish your name to be used by other carefully selected organizations for promotional purposes, please tick this box ☐